Mind-Shifting Imagery
Image Guidance for Life Coaches

Elizabeth-Anne Stewart

2018

This book presents the use of imagery as a tool for life coaching, spiritual direction and other forms of personal guidance with emotionally healthy clients; the author does not intend her work to be used as a substitute for medical or psychiatric protocols, or to be used with clients who are dealing with mental illness or emotional trauma. In the event that you use the information in this book in such a way as to harm yourself or someone else, the author assumes no responsibility for your actions.

Library of Congress Cataloging in Publication (CIP) data

Stewart, Elizabeth-Anne. 1951—
Mind-Shifting Imagery: Image Guidance for Life Coaches/ Elizabeth-Anne Stewart

ISBN-13:

978-1721576302

ISBN-10:

1721576304

Author's Portrait: Ola Orlikowska
Cover Photo/ Design: Elizabeth-Anne Stewart
www.artfulphotographer.com

www.elizabeth-annestewart.com; www.embracingpossibility.com

DEDICATION

To Martha

Weaver, story-teller and spiritual guide,

In gratitude for years of sacred listening

And for cradling me ever so tightly

In your heart-cloth...

CONTENTS

ACKNOWLEDGEMENTS

This little book and its author are indebted to the Administration and students of the *Institute for Life Coach Training* (ILCT). In the first place, Dean of Students, Ellen Neiley Ritter, has offered unwavering support in my journey from spiritual director/theologian to life coach. Ellen, your willingness to take me on as faculty and to go through all the paperwork involved in gaining ICF approval for my three courses— including *Image Guidance for Life Coaches*— has been remarkable. Director of Student Services, Kelly Adams, and Executive Director, Amy Jones – you have both been extraordinarily helpful, patient, and flexible. I have barraged you with complexities and special requests, and you have always been most gracious. And ILCT Founder, Pat Williams— what a privilege to have you as my "mentor coach!" I have learned so much from you, not only in our tele-mentoring sessions but also through your books, one of which (the heaviest!) traveled back and forth to Malta with me on several occasions when I was studying for the BCC.

Then I must thank my former ILCT students who have been such a joy to teach and learn from, especially: Sophie Fong, Stephen Kong, Bianka Krueger, Betty Morton and Jess Ryan. Thank you for allowing me to use your *Image Guidance* case studies in this book!

And, last but not least, I so deeply appreciate the many volunteer hours shared with Carolyn Johnson Dike, Sr. Dolores Lytle, CSA, Betty Morton, and Ola Orlikowska— it was so helpful to work with you on coaching applications for *Image Guidance* as I shifted the focus of my process from therapy to life coaching.

To all of you and to anyone whose kindness I have overlooked, please accept my heartfelt thanks!

FOREWORD

By Dr. Patrick Williams

Master Certified Coach, Board Certified Coach, and author of many books, including his roadmap for authentic living, *Getting Naked: On Being Emotionally Transparent at the Right Time, the Right Place, and with the Right Person.*

Elizabeth-Anne Stewart has spent decades in various professional identities of therapist, minister, spiritual director, and life coach, always bringing unique tools of her trade to the relationship. Elizabeth-Anne (Liz) is passionate about the power of accessing the unconscious when working with clients in a helping or coaching relationship.

Clients in any life transition, are seeking new awareness, which leads to new information, and that leads to new choices in behaviors, relationships, and new understandings of the journey at hand.

I have used the power of imagery from dreams, or from guided or directed imagery in both therapy and decades of coaching. The meaning that can be discovered behind images, however accessed, is often surprising and may even be transformational. There are times the images may have an emotional energy to them and the potential to be disturbing. But the goal is always to be illuminating, and the importance of a trained guide is paramount.

In **Mind-Shifting Imagery: Image Guidance for Life Coaches,** Liz offers a wealth of information, research citations, transcripts from sessions and clear distinctions on the variety of ways that imagery can be used in coaching without shifting into the world of psychotherapy or psychiatry.

She presents descriptions of the world of imagery from the world of art and literature and then the world of imagery in our own minds. Imagery guidance often leads to breakthroughs, and Liz includes such use in personal guidance, relationship challenges, healing from trauma or grief or loss, and then includes ways and means for incorporating imagery work in the corporate workplace.

As Liz states: "Image Guidance is a powerful tool designed to help clients access their own inner wisdom."

Indeed! In coaching we embrace the viewpoint that clients have the answers to their challenges within; they just don't know it or recognize yet. And in the process of coaching with a committed and trained listener, clients have opportunities to say what they have not said, and think what they have not yet thought, out loud. That often evokes insight and ideas for what's next to get to what is wanted or desired.

The use of imagery in the elegant and careful way that Liz covers in this book, allows an even deeper access to what is not yet known that is usually hidden somewhere in the unconscious. Through imagery work, coaches can make the unknown become known. And that can be transformational!

If you are a coach, therapist or some sort of life guide or catalyst, read this book and keep it handy as a guide for times when you feel stuck with a particular client or situation, or even to instill new creativity and energy into your work as a life coach.

PREFACE

In the early 1990's, I was immersed in the symbolic imagination, both in my teaching at *DePaul University* where I held a joint appointment with University Ministry and Religious Studies, and in free-lance work as a spiritual director. I learned that the imagination is one of the "places" where we encounter God and self in powerful ways; that it is in this sanctuary that we listen most attentively, feel most deeply, become most creative and receive the greatest clarity. I also learned that, for many, accessing this dimension of self is a challenge. Their rational self tells them that journeying into the imagination is child's play; or fear convinces them that the imagination is filled with terrifying specters that could turn life upside down. Instead of taking the mysterious journey inwards, they remain on the surface, satisfied with what is safe, rote and predictable.

Towards the end of an internship in spiritual direction, my fascination with the symbolic had led me to develop a process for accessing the unconscious that I named *"Image Guidance."* This allowed clients the opportunity to observe their own spontaneous images, to dialogue with them and discover life-changing possibilities. Through my explorations—mostly with faculty, staff and students at *DePaul*— I found that images function much like dreams in their ability to heal, guide and illumine. Over time, I amassed a series of case studies which Paulist Press published as *Image Guidance: A Tool for Spiritual Direction* (1992) and *Image Guidance and Healing* (1994).

Image Guidance is a powerful tool designed to help clients access their own inner wisdom. Though it doesn't replace conventional interventions, it can help us explore the roots of our issues and find strategies for dealing with them. Through imagery, we begin to understand the causes of illnesses, negative attitudes, addictions, and problematic behavior patterns. We can prepare for difficult or unpleasant medical procedures, personal confrontations or challenging situations; discern what is most life-giving when several choices present themselves; and live in harmony with situations which cannot be changed such as terminal illness, permanent disability, or irreversible loss. At the same time, the process can help us understand and deepen our relationships with God, self and others. The applications of this process are as varied as life itself. I have helped individuals re-enter their dreams, return to specific moments in their childhoods, imagine a new future, reduce physical symptoms, and find courage to deal with the inevitable challenges which present themselves.

In addition to working extensively with clients, I began presenting my research and providing training for various organizations across the country and beyond; these included *The Illinois Nurses Association; The National Association of Catholic Therapists (ACT); The Office of Ministry Formation, Archdiocese of Chicago; Resurrection Hospital* (chaplains); *American Association for the Study of Mental Imagery; Catholic Theological Union (CTU); Spiritual Directors International (SDI); C.G. Jung Institute, Chicago; Queens Retreat House, Saskatoon, Canada; Lutheran School of Theology in Chicago (LSTC); St. Xavier University, Chicago; and St. Scholastica Priory, Duluth, MN.*

Then came a change of direction – or, to be more precise, a new way of working with both imagery and clients. I became credentialed as a life coach and began teaching courses in spiritually-based life coaching for the *Institute for Life Coach Training (ILCT);* one of my courses just happened to be *Image Guidance for Life Coaches.* Although **Image Guidance** is a therapeutic process, I realized it had applications for life coaching which would be fully aligned with the *International Coach*

Federation's core competencies and Code of Ethics. Used briefly, as a forward-focusing tool rather than as a strategy for re-visiting the past, **Image Guidance** offers a doorway into self-knowledge (*I know who I am*) and self-awareness (*I understand my dreams, desires, fantasies, motivations and purpose, as well as the limiting beliefs that are stopping me from living the life I want to lead*).

Image Guidance is not a "coaching method," but it gives life coaches another "tool of the trade" which they can use on certain occasions for accessing the imagination and for accompanying their clients in ways that are safe and enlightening. Though there are many ways of using imagery to open up coaching possibilities and to bring about dramatic "mind-shifts," **Image Guidance** provides a process for doing so. Applications include, but are not limited to:

- Helping clients identify and describe emotions such as fear, frustration, excitement, enthusiasm;
- Assisting clients to identify "blocks" to their success, thereby reducing their negative energy, and allowing them to become unstuck;
- Assisting clients to imagine new possibilities and outcomes and to work towards these goals;
- Helping clients to prioritize, take action and evaluate;
- Affirming clients' hopes and dreams while re-enforcing their belief in self;
- Encouraging clients to accept new positions of leadership or areas of professional or personal responsibility etc.

This little book is designed for life coaches as an introduction to the use of **Image Guidance** in life coaching. I hope you find it useful!

INTRODUCTION

So what exactly is **"Image Guidance"** and how does it differ from **Guided Imagery** or the **Active Imagination**? All three processes involve the suspension of disbelief so that an image or series of images can lead us into a fictitious world in which "something happens." The client, for want of a better term, goes on a journey that holds some gift or revelation. A willing participant, this client often experiences heightened emotions and, in some cases, enters into an altered state of consciousness or condition resembling a hypnotic state. What actually happens depends on the client's 1) susceptibility to the power of imagery and 2) ability to relate to the imaginative content.

In the case of **Guided Imagery**, the imaginative journey is controlled by an external authority such as a meditation leader, digital recording or member of an "alternative" medical team. Typically, "live" **Guided Imagery** (as opposed to digitally-led imagery) takes place in a group setting in which participants are invited to close their eyes, focus on their breathing and relax. There may be soft music in the background or the gentle sound of birds chirping or running water, perhaps from a stream or waterfall. When the room is quiet, the leader speaks slowly and soothingly, inviting the group to leave behind the present moment and to begin an imaginative journey. The leader's voice, in fact, is almost hypnotic, and a skilled guide can modulate his or her voice in such a way that participants often experience an altered state of consciousness, one akin to being hypnotized.

The possibilities for this imaginative journey are endless, but typically, the guide leads the group into an experience of descent as this enables each participant to access the unconscious dimensions of self; simply imagining going down a ladder or staircase into subterranean depths helps clients to get in touch with forgotten or repressed dreams and fears. Then begins the narrative.

Very often there is a wisdom-figure in the cave with some revelation to share, or there may be a buried treasure which each participant must discover. The leader provides instructions which can range from asking the wisdom-figure a specific question to opening a treasure box which holds some secret or surprise. Eventually, the leader instructs the group to ascend to level ground and return to waking consciousness. It is not uncommon for participants to fall asleep during the experience or to return to the present moment feeling disoriented. When leading this type of imagery exercise, I find that while there is a handful of people who simply cannot "get into" the experience, most participants emerge with new understanding, less tension and anxiety and more energy. Though I may have imposed an imaginary journey on the group, each individual has a unique experience to share, shaped by his or her issues, associations, memories and reactions.

For several decades now, **Guided Imagery** has been used by medical practitioners to diagnose disease, alleviate symptoms, reverse chronic conditions and prepare patients for unpleasant or painful procedures, even for death. Just as stress and negative thinking can bring about disease, so positive imagery can affect physiology in positive ways. As early as 1929, studies demonstrated that "if one thinks intensively about a particular body movement, the appropriate motor neurons are activated" – hence mentally rehearsing swinging a golf club can trigger the muscles involved to become active (Achterberg 114). Apparently, imagery can affect everything from heart rate to blood pressure, from breath regulation to pain management. In her seminal work, *Imagery in Healing: Shamanism and Modern Medicine*, Jeanne Achterberg writes:

It is the interrelatedness among neurons and their activities that is critical to the assumption that imagery serves as an integrative mechanism between mental and physical processes. The brain areas associated with image storage, when sufficiently activated by thought (such as occurs when vivid, powerful images are created), can theoretically cause enough neurons to fire repeatedly, so the message reverberates through the brain. (120)

I experienced this interrelatedness between imagery and brain function many years ago when I was giving a family retreat at the U.S. Air Base in Aviano, Italy. After one of the sessions, a woman asked to speak to me privately. It turned out that her eight-year-old son, Alex, had lost the use of his right arm which had been severed, then re-attached, following a freak accident. The surgery had gone well, leaving the medical team confused as to why the boy's arm was still paralyzed a year later. Before the surgery, however, his mother had overheard a doctor say that the child's arm would never function again.

"Could that be the problem?" she asked me. "I think he heard this, too!"

I agreed to see Alex though I had never used imagery with a child before. Intuitively, I knew his mother was right in her suspicions.

"I want you to close your eyes and imagine that your arm is a tree branch that has dried up and lost its greening power," I told him.

"Now imagine that there is sap running through the branch, right from your shoulder, all the way down your upper arm, past your elbow, towards your wrist, across your hand and right to the very tips of your fingers. This sap is bringing new life to your branch which will now be able to move in the wind. When you open your eyes, you will see that your branch is alive again."

As I finished speaking, I noticed that Alex was staring at his hand. His arm hadn't moved, but his fingers and thumb had uncurled from their frozen position and were slowly stretching outwards.

"See!" I said. "The sap has reached your fingertips!"

Unfortunately, after my return to Chicago, I had no further contact with Alex; however, it was clear to me that a course of physiotherapy would eventually help him regain full use of his arm. The fact that he had witnessed movement in his hand was the "mind changer" that he needed.

While **Guided Imagery** depends upon an external guide, the **Active Imagination** is both self-directed and spontaneously occurring. However, it is not the mere daydreaming of a passive spectator but involves conscious participation in the symbolic dramas that flit before our eyes. Barbara Hannah, a student of Jung's, describes the **Active Imagination** as "a very individual and even lonely undertaking," one that is intensely private (12). For her, even the presence of another person in the room would become a deterrent, no matter how well she knew the person.

As I explained in *Image Guidance and Healing,* Jungian analysts regard the **Active Imagination** as the most powerful tool for exploring the unconscious:

> The ego actually goes into the inner world, walks, talks, confronts and argues, makes friends and fights with the persons it finds there.

You consciously take part in the drama in your imagination. You engage with other actors in conversation, exchange viewpoints, go through adventures together and eventually learn something from each other.… The "I" must enter into the imaginative act as intensely as it would if it were an external physical experience. Although it is a symbolic experience, it is still a real experience involving real feelings. (Johnson 140-141)

Personally, I don't encourage the use of the **Active Imagination** with anyone who is dealing with recent trauma, illness or loss, or with those who suffer from depression or mental illness. When one goes into the unconscious, anything can surface. What might seem like a simple imaginative exercise can end with terrifying imagery and even the risk of a psychotic break. This is why the presence of a guide is so essential. Barbara Hannah cautions:

Properly used, the method of Active Imagination can be of the greatest help in keeping our balance and in exploring the unknown; but misunderstood and indulged in, rather than regarded as a piece of scientific *hard work*, it can release forces in the unconscious that can overcome us. (6)

As in the case of **Guided Imagery**, **Image Guidance** involves the "live" presence of an external guide of the human variety (as opposed to a digital recording). Instead of relying on pre-fabricated images or a "one style fits all" approach, **Image Guidance** bears a resemblance to the **Active Imagination** in that it involves the client's own unique imagery. Where it differs, however, is that the client is accompanied by a guide throughout the experience. The role of the guide is to facilitate but not control, to invite rather than direct. By asking powerful questions, making suggestions, offering support and encouragement and keeping the client focused, the guide serves as "midwife" for whatever revelations surface. It is the guide's task to lead the client into the imagery and to bring the experience to an end, when appropriate. With the help of the guide, the client begins a conversation with the images that surface, repeating out loud *what* is said and describing *how* it is said. The images direct and the guide encourages the client to respond.

In therapeutic contexts, **Image Guidance** can be a lengthy, complex process that may run anywhere from 30 minutes to several hours. The journey often takes client and guide back into the distant past where family dynamics can be re-visited, re-enacted and given different endings. Clients have the opportunity to confront abusers, destroy "old tapes," heal gaping wounds and find and dispense forgiveness.

Nothing is impossible as we travel back in time and the past becomes present once more. I have taken clients back to the high chair and beyond, helping them understand the family dynamics that helped shape their present realities, even if this means a long journey into the past. In one case, **Image Guidance** helped a student understand why she fainted every time her mother visited campus; it turned out that when she was an infant, she developed a high fever and her mother's panic so terrified her that she fainted on the spot. After that, she fainted whenever she sensed her mother was upset about anything. Through imagery, we solved the problem in less than an hour.

In another situation, a Holocaust survivor was able to go back decades to when she was four years old, and her parents had left her with a Christian family so they could go into hiding. Though the family reunited at the end of the war and though she led a "normal" life for many decades, suddenly, in her late seventies, she began hitting a little girl in her care, without provocation. Through our work together, she learned that she was projecting her unspoken childhood rage onto the child who was about the same age she had been when her parents left her behind.

In yet another case, a middle-aged woman wanted to find relief from the migraines she had endured for fifteen years; together, we journeyed back in time to the very first migraine, discovering that it coincided with the client's having had an abortion. She had never faced her feelings of guilt and deep regret, and though she seldom thought about the abortion, the reality of that traumatic event was still embodied in her. As Jung points out, what is not dealt with, doesn't go away; it is simply out of sight.

Through **Image Guidance**, a focus on the future is also possible, and this is where Life Coaching comes in. Any focus on the past runs the risk of becoming a therapy session in which the client concentrates on the roots of his or her woundedness. It is possible, of course, to invite clients to go back to a time when they felt fulfilled, happy and productive so they can discover the happy formula for these positive feelings. I call this identifying "touchstone experiences" and believe they are as important in coaching as they are in therapy. Such experiences remind clients of their strengths, abilities, courage, resourcefulness and survival power; in short, they help move the client's agenda forwards. Typically, however, I would recommend a forward-focus for life coaching sessions.

Image Guidance allows the client to imagine new possibilities, explore options, diffuse negative situations and clarify complexities. Again, the guide serves as a companion and facilitator, helping make sense of all that the imagery reveals. By asking powerful questions and using **Image Guidance** as a brief intervention, the coach assists the client to go deeper, feel more intensely, understand more clearly and be more authentic. The steps are as follows but can be adapted as needed:

1. Guide and client converse about the presenting issue or situation so that the guide has a full understanding of the client's agenda.
2. The guide asks leading questions until the client can "picture" the situation through an image or series of images.
3. The guide leads the client into a deep state of relaxation through breathing and relaxation techniques, inviting him/her to focus only on the image.
4. The guide gives verbal directions to assist the client interact with the imagery according to his or her comfort level.
5. The client converses with the image while sharing with the guide what s/he has seen, heard and felt.
6. When the client has received sufficient feedback, the guide then facilitates the return to waking consciousness.
7. When the client is re-oriented to the present moment, the guide discusses the experience with him or her and helps evaluate all that has happened.

In the next few chapters, I will explain how each of these steps can be used in coaching contexts. Again, **Image Guidance** is not a method of coaching but a tool to be used selectively and carefully so that clients can experience a "mind shift" and cross the great divide that separates them from where they are today and where they hope to be tomorrow.

CHAPTER ONE:
PITFALLS & POSSIBILITIES

Whenever I conduct a training session in **Image Guidance**, I am careful to point out both the power of the process and its potential dangers. Obviously, using imagery for brief, targeted interventions to help a coaching client gain clarity, perspective or a sense of direction is very different than a lengthy session in which someone goes back in time to confront lurking "demons." In the first case, the brevity of the experience is itself a safety control, as is the desired outcome. In a coaching context, the client is looking towards the future and the best way to get there. Used as a therapeutic intervention, however, **Image Guidance** facilitates re-entry into the past where painful memories are likely to be activated. Moreover, the longer we descend into the unconscious, the more we might discover that puts us in touch with raw emotions. What a client encounters imaginatively feels only too real and it is largely the presence of the guide that allows him or her to navigate past experiences in a manner that is healing rather than devastating. At the same time, the guide closely monitors the symbolic drama through careful questioning and can re-direct the imagery or bring the client back to the present, if necessary.

Another way of looking at differences between the use of imagery in coaching and in therapy is to examine typical client responses. When the client is focusing on creating a positive future, as in coaching, s/he is engaged with planning, adapting and organizing data; emotions are also present, but these support the client's forward-thinking agenda; in contrast, when the client focuses on unpleasant past events, then the desire to flee, take flight and find safety may surface. Also, if layers of repressed material are brought to light too quickly, the client might experience acute emotional distress. All this, of course, must be avoided in a coaching session.

For reasons stated above, **Image Guidance** as a therapeutic tool is best left to those who have the professional skills to work with past tense traumas and "unsolved mysteries." This does not necessarily involve a PhD in psychology, but the guide must be highly intuitive, exceptionally compassionate and well-versed in the realm of symbols and archetypes. I, myself, am not a trained psychotherapist; it is my decades-long background in theology, spiritual direction, mythology and literature that has immersed me in the symbolic imagination. Even so, I stay within what I consider to be safe parameters. There have been times when I have worked with a client only when his or her psychotherapist has been present; there are also clients with whom I have refused to work, especially if they are clinically depressed, have experienced recent trauma or are taking mind-altering medications. This is why it is so essential to screen potential clients and to have a referral system in place, should the client require psychological follow-up. In *Image Guidance: A Tool for Spiritual Direction*, I write:

> There are *directees* I regularly see with whom I have never used **Image Guidance** and with whom I am unlikely to do so. These individuals are usually very insecure— so much so that their grip on life is tentative at best and any probing into the unconscious becomes an existential threat…. There are also people who are good candidates for **Image Guidance** but who have difficulties with particular issues. These issues can cause resistance, and resistance, in turn, can break down the process. (12-13)

My concern regarding the safe use of imagery may seem excessive, but there is a backstory which I pieced together after its tragic conclusion. Many years ago, a childhood friend began practicing meditation. This, in itself, was not extraordinary, but John had come from a very abusive home and was later sexually abused at a religious boarding school. His mother had died when he was a toddler, and his father had always blamed him for his mother's death; had John not been born, reasoned his dad, his mother would never have developed cancer. John had neither faith nor faith community; he simply practiced meditation on his own, and when he began hearing voices, there was no one he could turn to for guidance.

When he shared with his wife that the voices were God speaking to him and that these voices wanted him to atone for a life he had taken in a previous lifetime, she had no idea how to respond. By the time she realized he needed help, it was too late: John had taken his own life to "atone" for his supposed previous act of violence.

It had been many years since I had connected with John, but hearing the news, I tracked down his wife whom I had never met. In talking to her, I realized that for John, suicide had been a "religious act," an act of obedience. For the first time in his life, he had found happiness and had everything to live for; "God," however, had other plans for him and he followed instructions. Apparently, his wife had also believed that "God" was speaking to him, hence her lack of action. What was clear to me was that "God" was the voice of his father who had blamed him for his mother's cancer. As a spiritual guide, I always ask clients to distinguish between what is life-giving and what is death-dealing, reminding them that God always calls us to life. There was no such guidance to help John discern the source of his voices.

Anything can surface from the unconscious – voices, images, repressed memories, archetypal material. For some individuals, a descent into the unconscious is dangerous and should only take place under the skilled care of a psychotherapist or someone else who has the training and ability to guide in these waters. As a university minister at DePaul, I kept a framed photo on my bookshelf to remind me of this: it depicted a heavily vegetated Floridian waterway with two poles jutting out of the water; on one pole was the head of a mannequin and, on the other, a sign which ominously said, *"Welcome, If You Have Webbed Feet."* To navigate the unconscious and to dare guide another into that territory, we must have webbed feet, spiritually speaking.

But back to coaching! Again, to be ethically and safely employed, imagery in life coaching must serve the client's agenda. This starts with the *Coaching Agreement*. Coaches have many tools and methods to choose from, and I believe that the *Coaching Agreement* is the first place to name them. One of the clauses that I include in the *Agreement* simply states: *"I understand that my coach will use a variety of strategies and techniques to advance my coaching agenda; these may include but are not limited to storytelling, brief experiences with imagery and artwork."*

Another clause to which my clients must agree distinguishes between coaching and psychotherapy: *"I understand that life coaching is not a substitute for psychotherapy and is not intended to treat mental or emotional disorders; moreover, if I am working with a mental health professional, I will only enter into a coaching relationship after consulting both my therapist and coach."*

My *Welcome Package* also includes a detailed questionnaire which will guide me as to whether I should use **Image Guidance** with a particular client. Any suggestion that the client may require therapy in addition to coaching is enough to make me steer clear of imagery work. Perhaps I am excessively careful in this regard, but, potential liability issues aside, there is my very real concern for the well-being of the client: while imagery may be a powerful tool to use with *most* clients, it may not be a safe tool for *every* client. Having said this, I suspect that this holds true for most of the tools in our coaching "toolbox," not just **Image Guidance.**

How the coach "shows up" is another ethical consideration where the use of imagery is concerned. Though professional ethics dictate that the coach should always be awake and alert, ready to listen not just to words but to the spaces between words and their underlying meaning, any coach who intends to use imagery must be well-rested and in a state of personal balance. Whether the coaching session is conducted in person or by telephone, active listening is essential. The coach cannot be distracted, even for a minute. Every gesture, every facial expression, every shift in posture, every change in tone or speech patterns, every period of silence – all this must be present to the coach.

Where imagery is concerned, everything is important. The coach must pay attention to the client's emotional state as well as to what is happening inside the coach. During phone calls, I often close my eyes to accompany my client's encounter with images. Aware of my feelings and those of the client, I am less likely to impose my interpretation on the imagery, more likely to allow the imagery to reveal its own meaning. When the client is physically present, I tend to keep my eyes open, watching for any "Ah ha!" moments, potential breakthroughs or changes in facial expression. When I first developed the process, I discovered that "my ability to listen extended beyond hearing to *feeling* what the seeker was saying" (*Image Guidance: A Tool for Spiritual Direction* 10). As a result, the presence I communicated was that of the empathic listener; this allowed me to enter the experience as participant rather than detached observer: "Intuitively, I knew what questions to ask and what to leave unsaid, when to be silent and when to speak, when to intervene and when to let the image accomplish its own work" (11).

As an active listener, the coach will know when an "**Image Guidance** moment" is likely to be helpful. The client's use of metaphorical language is the first signal that such a moment would be appropriate. In the following example, Brian, a project manager with an engineering company, had been discussing his growing sense of alienation in the workplace. He had expected a promotion, but someone was hired for the position from outside the company. Things were not going well. Here is a rough transcription of our phone session:

BRIAN: "I feel dwarfed by this guy, He's half my age, has half my credentials, yet he's the rising star in the company now."

COACH: "That must be really frustrating! So if he's rising, what's happening to you?

BRIAN: "I'm on the fringes— upper management listens only to him, and he definitely doesn't appreciate anything I have to contribute. In fact, my presence seems to annoy him."

COACH: "This sounds like an awkward situation – can't be very pleasant for you. What would you like to focus on? There are several directions we can explore here."

BRIAN: "I want to look at how I can get along with him. Perhaps there's something I need to change, so we can actually get to work together."

COACH: "With your permission, I would first like to go back to a word you used earlier. You said you felt 'dwarfed' –what do mean by that?"

BRIAN: "What the word says – I mean, I feel entirely eclipsed, small, overshadowed, irrelevant, invisible…."

COACH: "I'd like to focus on this word for a few minutes. I invite you to close your eyes and to picture yourself standing next to your new boss. When you're both in focus, without opening your eyes, describe what you can see."

BRIAN: "We're standing back to back, as if about to begin a duel, but neither of us is holding a weapon. In fact, we have our arms folded across our chests in a kind of executive position, heads half turned to face an audience or possibly a camera. We're both wearing business attire, but he is much taller – in fact, I seem to be shrinking."

COACH: "So you're shrinking as you describe this?

BRIAN: "Yes. He's getting taller and more muscular – now he has bulging biceps like Popeye in the old spinach commercials."

COACH: "And what is happening to you?"

BRIAN: "Still shrinking. I think he's going to stomp on me."

COACH: "What can you say to him that will make him less aggressive?"

BRIAN: "No – nothing. He has this sadistic gleam in his eyes as if he can't wait to destroy me."

COACH: "Before the shrinking Brian disappears, ask him if there's anything you can change in your behavior to make your boss friendlier or less aggressive. Then let me know what you have heard."

BRIAN: "He says nothing. He's telling me there's absolutely nothing I can do. He says my boss doesn't want me around because I make him look inept. Everyone knows he's not qualified for the job."

COACH: "So what does shrinking Brian recommend?"

BRIAN: "He says there is no way I will ever get along with this guy. He advises me to start looking for a new job."

COACH: "Brian, you can open your eyes now. What did you learn about how you can get along with your boss?"

BRIAN: "That it would be a waste of time! He wants me out of there. Change of agenda here— I need to explore next steps!"

As guide, I could have gone with either the image of a rising star or with the image of my client being dwarfed. Either way, I believe we would have come to the same conclusion. The unconscious communicates via symbols, and if one symbol fails to convey the message, then another may work more effectively. As a result of our coaching session, Brian began to search for a new job. He was given notice shortly after our conversation, but the company gave him a generous severance package and the opportunity to work with HR to find alternative employment. Our coaching session not only prepared him for his dismissal but also reassured him that there was nothing further he could have done to shift his bad rapport with his boss.

Regarding the seven-step process I outlined in the Introduction, six of the steps were present in this brief **Image Guidance** intervention. The presenting issue was Brian's coaching agenda, namely, his desire to improve his relationship with his boss. Instead of asking Brian to come up with an image, I focused on a metaphor that he presented in conversation— the image of being "dwarfed." I omitted step three— leading the client into the unconscious via deep breathing techniques— and instead went directly to steps four and five: facilitating the client's interaction with imagery via verbal directions while monitoring the feedback the client receives. I then asked Brian to open his eyes, so we could process what he had learned from his images.

Step three is essential in a therapeutic context; it is through breath work while focusing intently on an image that the client enters an altered state of consciousness, at times even a hypnotic state. For reasons stated earlier, this would be inappropriate for life coaching. Moreover, step six following a journey back in time involves more than asking a client to open his or her eyes. If the client has descended into the unconscious, the return journey needs to be carefully orchestrated. Before bringing someone back to waking consciousness, I first provide assurances that the issues of the past do not have to mar present or future; slowly, I speak words of affirmation, encouragement and hope, sometimes inviting the client to repeat self-affirmations such as, *"I have all the courage I need to face this challenge,"* or, *"I will never allow anyone to abuse me again."* Or sometimes, if clients have had an amazingly beautiful experience of harmony, reconciliation or healing, I invite them to linger with the experience and to open their eyes when they are ready to do so. I sit in silence and wait.

Regardless of how therapeutic **Image Guidance** clients return to the present, they tend to feel tired and disoriented, perhaps even dizzy. For this reason, **Image Guidance** healing sessions are by appointment only in an office setting where I can observe the client's responses. I ask clients to block out 1-2 hours and to agree to take public transportation after the session, or else have someone drive them home. In contrast, adapting **Image Guidance** for life coaching presents none of these issues. The transcript of my session with Brian reflects a brief exchange with a powerful outcome and no side effects!

Talking to an image and relaying what the image says back to a coach is not for everyone. There is the element of the ridiculous in the **Image Guidance** process, and not every client (or coach!) is going to want to risk absurdity. Brian was, fortunately, familiar with my process and understood that there was insight to be gained by playing along with his imagery. Had he not experienced **Image Guidance** before, I would have interjected a brief explanation, something like this:

COACH: "With your permission, I would first like to go back to a word you used earlier. You said you felt 'dwarfed' –what do mean by that?"

BRIAN: "What the word says – I mean, I feel entirely eclipsed, small, overshadowed, irrelevant, invisible…."

COACH: "I'd like to focus on this word for a few minutes, using imagery as a tool for moving forward. Let me explain. When you used the adjective, "dwarfed," I sensed that it has some literal meanings as well as figurative ones. With your permission, I would like you to have a conversation with the image of you being dwarfed. I know this sounds strange, but if you are willing to humor me a little, I think we'll find some of the answers you're seeking. Basically, what I need you to do is to close your eyes and to picture yourself being dwarfed. I will then have a brief series of questions for you, including ones that you ask your image. You will then let me know what you see and hear, and we can process the answers together. If you would rather talk this through than use imagery, that's fine with me. What do you think?"

BRIAN: "Suppose my image doesn't communicate?"

COACH: "It will."

BRIAN: "And can it really shed light on my relationship with my boss?"

COACH: "I believe so – that's why I'm suggesting this, but it's entirely up to you."

BRIAN: "Okay, then, but I feel a bit of an idiot."

COACH: "I understand. Everyone does first time around. If you don't find this useful, we'll forget about imagery in the future."

BRIAN: "Okay, It's a deal, then."

Had Brian been a new client, I would not have used **Image Guidance** with him, no matter how beneficial it might have been. Building trust and intimacy in the coaching relationship is foundational to effective coaching. I was only able to spring this unusual coaching strategy on Brian because we had already worked together for a period of several months, and he trusted my ability to coach him; he also knew that his well-being was my priority and that I always followed his agenda, even if there were seeming detours, every now and again.

Using **Image Guidance** successfully in coaching contexts involves knowing when to use it, with whom and for what purpose. It is to be used sparingly and appropriately and can never become an end in itself. The coach must resist the temptation to go back to the past (unless for what I described earlier as a "touchstone moment") or to prolong the session by letting the imagery take over. Rather, the coach must be fully present, listening actively while taking the opportunity to ask powerful questions, request clarifications, mirror what is being said and then invite the client to interpret what he or she has experienced.

When listening to an image unfold, I often intuitively know what light it is shedding on a particular situation; however, I never impose my interpretation on the client. Instead, I might ask open-ended questions such as, *"What did you learn from your image?"* and *"Is there another way of looking at what this might mean?"* Or, *"What does this image want of you?"* The only time I could see myself disagreeing with a client's interpretation would be if the image advocated actions or attitudes that go against the client's core values and which might have destructive outcomes. So far, in thirty years of using this process, this has never been an issue, but it is one that I'm aware could surface without warning, at any moment. This why the coach cannot be distracted at any point in the **Image Guidance** process.

But what if the coach *is* feeling distracted, or what if the client is not in an emotionally-safe place to work with imagery? Life "happens" and our perfect selves do not always show up on schedule. My strategy, then, is to ask the client ***to draw the image*** and to see what it reveals. Going back to Brian, he could have drawn himself being dwarfed by his boss. In a phone session, he could then have described what he saw in the picture, providing details about facial expression, posture, clothing style, settings and other variables. In an office setting, we could have analyzed the drawing together. In each case, I, the coach, could have asked similar questions to the ones I asked when he was working with **Image Guidance**.

COACH: "So how does it feel to be so small when you used to be the group leader?" **OR**

COACH: "What does your boss's smirk tell you about his plans for the future?" **OR**

COACH: "What does your self-portrait show you about the way this work situation is having an impact on you physically and emotionally?"

Making sure clients always have access to paper, pens, markers or crayons is one way of ensuring that no metaphor is wasted, even if the use of **Image Guidance** might be inadvisable. You may even want to include this as a requirement in your coaching agreement.

CHAPTER TWO:
THE SYMBOLIC IMAGINATION

Myths, symbols and metaphors are doorways into the unconscious. Whether we're aware of this or not, we're constantly drawing on mythical themes, symbols, and metaphors whenever we attempt to express ourselves in speech or writing. Sometimes, the images which surface are commonly used clichés while, at others, they are uniquely original. When a client is "fighting an uphill battle," or "getting too close to the edge," or feels "off-base," or is "on a merry-go-round," or is "taking a gamble," or is "walking on egg shells," or is "on a roller-coaster," or is "buried under a mountain of shit," there are familiar metaphors for the coach to zone in on. In some cases, it is one image that predominates such as being "off-base." In others, the metaphor may have several components, such as "being buried under a mountain of shit." Unsavory as this metaphor might seem, it offers rich potential: "being buried" + "being under a mountain" + "being under a mountain of shit." Each phase of the metaphor is important: *How* did the client become buried and what is this experience like? *What* is burying the client alive – Activities? Possessions? Other people's expectations? Family responsibilities? *How* can the client gradually chip away at the mountain to reduce its weight? Is the mountain really a pile of shit or is this just the client's negative perception? If "shit" is involved, whose "shit" is it? *How* might "shit" be transformed to "gold"?

It takes creativity and heightened intuition on the part of the coach to know which images to pursue and which to leave alone. If time is an issue, I work with the image that holds the most energy. One of the most highly-charged images I have ever worked with surfaced during a religious retreat. One of the participants— a

Catholic nun— said she felt like *"A flattened worm that had just been run over on hot asphalt."* As you might imagine, this simile took several sessions to "unpack," but it provided a wealth of information regarding the participant's negative emotional space, her difficult relationship with her community and her wrestling with vocational issues.

Even more powerful are mythical and archetypal themes. The coach who is well-versed in myths, archetypes, and biblical stories is at an advantage here. Images of "flying too high" might trigger memories of the Icarus story; an ordinary citizen heroically taking on a corporate giant might remind us of David and Goliath; somebody who has multiple tasks ahead might be living the story of the *Labors of Hercules*; the client who is pushing hard and getting nowhere may be a modern-day Sisyphus.... If we listen carefully, we will encounter a world filled with dragon-slayers, riddle-solvers, bold rescuers, wounded kings, damsels in distress, evil queens, wastelands to redeem and mazes to conquer. At the same time, however, we must resist the temptation to assume that we know what a myth or symbol means: for one client, a garden might represent the Garden of Eden and a fall from grace, while, for another, it could symbolize the transformation of desert into agricultural land. "Mythical consciousness" can shape our responses in intuitive ways; however, it can also steer us away from exploring the client's unique interpretation.

Regardless of their origin, images can reveal much about a client's feelings, challenges, hopes for the future and so on. It is only natural, then, that "professional listeners" need to be attuned to the imagery that surfaces in clients' narratives. These images help us understand dimensions of their experience that would otherwise be inaccessible; in turn, this helps us form powerful questions which can lead clients into deeper discoveries and more heightened awareness. Take, for example, two versions of the following exchange:

COACH: "So what has happened since our last appointment?"

BRENDA: "Nothing much. I'm still doing a juggling act, but with a few more balls in the air and less ability to catch them."

COACH: "That sounds tough – I'd hoped you'd have some good news to share regarding your workload. Do you still want to focus on time management skills?"

BRENDA: "Yes."

In this exchange, the coach checks in with the client at the beginning of their session, but completely ignores her use of metaphor. True, the coach understands that Brenda has a heavy workload, but s/he misses the fact that she has taken on more responsibilities and is beginning to feel overwhelmed. The coach expresses empathy for the client and then, instead of providing agenda options, asks the client whether she wishes to work on their previously established agenda of time-management. Having been offered an invitation with a "Yes/No" response, Brenda agrees that to focus on time management would be a good use of her coaching session. The result? Missed opportunity!

Let's try a different approach:

COACH: "So what has happened since our last appointment?"

BRENDA: "Nothing much. I'm still doing a juggling act, but with a few more balls in the air and less ability to catch them."

COACH: "Oh no! You were already juggling six or seven activities last week! What new balls have come your way?"

BRENDA: "Well, in addition to planning conferences, facilities management and inventory control, I've now been put in charge of IT for all departments; moreover, I have three new interns to supervise."

COACH: "That's quite a mix of responsibilities!"

BRENDA: "You're telling me – this is not sustainable! Actually, this is what I would like to focus on today. I'm absolutely overwhelmed."

COACH: "I hear you, but let's take a look at your juggling act. If you are willing to do so, I'd like to focus on the image of you juggling. Close your eyes for a few minutes and then describe what this juggling act looks like so that I can imagine it as well."

BRENDA: "Well, I'm dressed in black, and there's no color anywhere. I'm in an empty room with white walls and no windows, and I'm heaving these grey balls into the air; the minute I catch one ball another one gets tossed into the mix – it's like I'm juggling 12 balls or more."

COACH: "What additional details can you give me about the way you look?"

BRENDA: "I have a blank stare, no emotions of any kind. I'm standing tall and straight and look as if I've become mechanical."

COACH: "What do you mean by that?"

BRENDA: "I'm on auto-pilot. I don't know what I'm doing, and I don't care."

COACH: "What don't you care about?"

BRENDA: "I know I'm going to drop the balls eventually, so the best thing is not to care. If I drop them, I'll be fired, so I have to prepare myself for the worst by not caring."

COACH: "Brenda, as you watch this imagery think of some advice you can give Brenda the Juggler. What might make her situation tolerable?"

BRENDA: "I would tell her she has to stop juggling."

COACH: "And how would that be possible?"

BRENDA: "She has to have a conversation with management and delegate some of her workload to the interns."

COACH: "Great! I think you're on the right track here! Let's talk about it!"

In this version, the coach again checks in with the client at the beginning of the session, but quickly utilizes Brenda's imagery with the question, *"What new balls have come your way?"* This single question demonstrates that the coach's emotions are aligned with those of the client, and that s/he has already entered the client's symbolic narrative. After receiving the clarification that was missing in the first version, the coach then leads Brenda into a brief experience of **Image Guidance** in which she can envision the full extent of her desperation, as well as a possible remedy. Note that the coach does not come up with solutions but allows the client to arrive at her own strategies. By participating in the imaginative experiences of the client, the coach is both objective guide and subjective participant. Commenting on this phenomenon in *Image Guidance and Healing*, I write:

> Even as I analyze the images which unfold before me, even as I observe the client's facial expressions and body language, even as I remember the context out of which the

> images developed, my emotions are highly involved in the client's narrative.
>
> I see what the client sees, I hear what the client hears, I feel what the client feels, but, at the same time, my professional self is at work, making connections, intuiting meaning, evaluating, facilitating, and making decisions about closure. (11)

As subjective participant, the coach bonds with the client, communicating empathy through his/her presence and not merely through words. The client feels heard, experiencing acceptance, understanding and encouragement. Client and coach can literally be said to be on the "same wave-length." Neuroscience research suggests that the deepest levels of communication happen when brains "couple" or connect through listening/speaking activities. Using MRI technology to record the brain activity of speakers and listeners engaged in conversation, Princeton University neuroscientists, Uri Hasson, Lauren J. Silbert and Greg J. Stephens, "used the speaker's spatiotemporal brain activity to model listeners' brain activity and found that the speaker's activity is spatially and temporally coupled with the listener's activity. This coupling vanishes when participants fail to communicate" (abstract). They also observed that while the listener's brain activity "mirrors the speaker's activity with a delay, we also find areas that exhibit predictive anticipatory responses." In fact, the greater the anticipatory coupling, the greater the understanding between speaker and listener. I would venture that this "anticipatory" quality of speech is present to an even stronger degree in the sharing of imagery and in the silence that falls between words.

This understanding of how listener/speaker brain activity can light up a coaching conversation sets the stage for deeper discoveries and more creative problem-solving in the context of a solid coaching relationship. Following a helpful experience with imagery, the client may be willing to examine aspects of the imagery that may have been overlooked first time around. In the second interaction between the coach and Brenda, for example, the sterility of the room in which Brenda is juggling is worth returning to, and the fact that she feels "mechanical" reveals much about her inner world.

The imagery has not only revealed Brenda's stress at work but also the impact of stress on her personal life and her personality. She has a "blank stare," is on "auto-pilot," and has "no emotions of any kind." All this offers a rich lead into what Brenda needs to avoid and the happier future awaiting her if she can end the cycle of juggling.

Learning how to work with imagery is not as hard as it might seem. The first challenge for the coach is that s/he must believe in the power of the symbol-using, symbol-making imagination to further the client's agenda. Without this belief, the coach will simply be dabbling in pictures, often confusing the client in the process. The starting point, then, is the self. We need to begin paying attention to the images that spontaneously show up in our lives, listening to what they have to say to us. During a creative writing class I was teaching recently, I asked my students if they had ever been directed by their symbols. One student shared how she had been all set to go out with her friends when she suddenly caught sight of an owl in a nearby tree. In her family, owls were considered bad omens, so she decided to stay home. She later found out that her friends had been arrested for armed robbery and drug use. Had she gone out with them, she, too, would have ended up in jail. Another student recalled seeing a magnificent purple butterfly shortly after a friend's death; the friend loved the color purple, and so the butterfly seemed to offer the assurance that she was at peace, "on the other side."

The example I shared was that of an institutional clock falling off the wall in a college classroom. I was teaching at a school in downtown Chicago that had no security measures in place. Gang members wandered freely, beating up whom they pleased, and one of my students –a vet with anger issues— seemed like a time-bomb ready to explode. One day, a faculty member poked her head around the door to warn me that other faculty had barricaded themselves in their offices because the angry student was insisting they convert his "F's" to "A's." At that precise moment, the clock fell. "A sign!" I said to myself. "Time's up! I'm out of here!" And I never went back

Dream symbols are another way of schooling ourselves in the riches of the imagination. Regular "dream work" immerses us in the unconscious where we can observe nocturnal dramas or actively participate in them. By observing our imagery, we can distinguish between the *Dream Ego* and the cast of minor characters, between what Jung described as *"the Shadow"* (repressed dreams, memories, and events) and the *Animus* (feminine soul) and *Anima* (masculine soul). We record every detail of the plot, without censorship, identify the theme and grow adept in understanding what it is the Dream requires of us. The more skilled we are in analyzing our dreams, the better we will navigate the symbols that manifest in our client's narratives.

Symbols that are universal in nature, spontaneously occurring in world myths, art, religions and literature, are especially powerful and can grip us —for better or worse—with extraordinary tenacity. The cast of archetypal characters includes the Holy Child, the

Savior, the Trickster, the Hero, the Liberator, the Magician, the Sage, the Wise Fool, the Lover, the Martyr, the Warrior, the Saint, the Healer…. Each of these images may be active at some point in our lives; sometimes, a cluster of archetypes governs us. Jung cautions against treating archetypes as "part of a mechanical system." For him, they are "pieces of life itself— images that are integrally connected to the living individual by the bridge of the emotions"(87). As living realities, archetypes have negative dimensions as well as positive ones. In *Jesus the Holy Fool*, I paraphrase the what Carol Pearson has said on the topic:

> The benign ruler, for example, can become an ogre tyrant; the magician who holds all things in balance can degenerate into an evil sorcerer; the sage can be an unfeeling judge; the caregiver can control others by making them feel guilty; the trickster can resort to cruel and gruesome strategies. Pearson explains that it is the addictive quality of each archetype that leads us into being possessed by the shadow. (16)

The coach who wishes to use **Image Guidance** with a client must also become familiar with myths and symbols – there is no way around this basic requirement. A first step is to read myths from various cultures and to notice similarities, as well as differences. Most cultures, for example, have heroic myths following the six phases of the Heroic Quest as outlined by Joseph Campbell: *The Call to Adventure, The Threshold of Adventure, The Road of Trials, Helpers Along the Way, The At-One-Ment (or Sacred Marriage or Quest for the Holy Grail)* and *The Return Journey.* Briefly put, these six phases represent 1) the call to leave behind old consciousness and sometimes an old location or occupation; 2) the call to begin the adventure, while combating outer and inner doubts and feelings of unworthiness; 3) the experience of profound suffering which allows the hero to prove his/her worthiness for the journey; 4) the various helpers (human, mythical, mystical, animal, etc.) who assist the hero survive the Road of Trials; 5) the experience of Unity or "At-One-Ment with God, Self and others, as well as with all creation; 6) the call to share what one has learned with some other individual or group.

When the coach can listen to a client's narrative and see reflections of these stages of the *Hero Quest*, then s/he is thinking mythically. The client's *Call to Adventure* may not be identical to the call of Jesus or the call of Buddha or the call of Martin Luther King Jr., but it may involve leaving behind the familiar and embarking on some great undertaking for which the client may feel totally unprepared. Similarly, just as these heroes may have had to struggle with negative voices or temptations before they could fully accept *The Call*, so the client may also have to struggle with fears, doubts, and negative feedback.

Precisely because of its universality and its inspirational dimensions, *The Hero Quest* is one of the most useful mythical paradigms to introduce into a coaching session. Even if this is the only myth with which the coach is familiar, it provides a wealth of insights:

> If those undergoing painful experiences can reflect on their lives from the vantage point of the heroic quest, how much easier it is to move beyond the pain and to channel one's energies into positive action! If, for example, one can see in situations of dissatisfaction or loss a call to high adventure, then limiting events can become bearable. If one can imagine that the blocks or obstacles lying ahead are dragons guarding the *Threshold of Adventure,* then the task of overcoming them is ennobling. If one has to lean upon helpers to survive, then the knowledge that this is a temporary phase of the heroic

quest provides the assurance that there will be a time when independence will be a possibility. And if *The Road of Trials* is seemingly without end, then to know that one is walking the path to increased consciousness at least offers a little comfort where perhaps there would be none. *(Image Guidance: A Tool for Spiritual Direction,* 47)

Watching movies with mythical themes is one way of developing the ability to recognize the mythical dimensions of a client's narrative. Like Sisyphus, the client may be struggling and getting nowhere; like Pandora, the client may have opened up a situation that has unpleasant consequences; like Jonah, the client may have been swallowed by darkness and may now be trapped in the belly of the great fish; like Moses, the client may be called to liberate co-workers from a situation of oppression; like Persephone, the client may have ventured into the underworld; like the wounded Fisher King, the client may be presiding over an arid land, waiting for the Holy Grail to bring relief …. Once the coach can recognize these themes in movies, s/he is more likely to be able to identify them in "real life" situations and to have the coaching agility to use them to advance the client's agenda.

The 1980's gave rise to countless commentaries on myths and archetypes which still have much to teach us to this day. Joseph Campbell, of course, was the master of mythical interpretation and inspiration, providing the groundwork for academic studies, pop psychology and even the movie industry (as in the case of *Star Wars*). Jeanne Achterberg focused on imagery and healing, while authors such as Robert Johnson, Jean Shinoda Bolen and Clarissa Pinkola Estes wrote extensively on masculine and feminine psychology. Then there were writers who explored the transformation of consciousness (Carol Pearson), the mythic imagination (Stephen Larsen), and the presence of what Jung termed as "the Shadow," that part of ourselves which has been repressed, silenced, discounted and ignored to our own detriment (Jeremiah Abrams and Connie Zweig). For any coach who wishes to further his or her understanding of the power of imagery, these authors provide a critical resource.

As a coach with a busy practice, you might find this suggestion unrealistic. Who, after all, has the time for such a reading list? Having taught *Myths, Signs and Symbols* at both a graduate level and undergraduate level and having written on the archetype of the *Holy Fool* for my dissertation in Theology, I have been fortunate enough to study this world in depth. It has not only helped form my personal consciousness but has worked to my professional advantage in spiritual direction, life coaching and teaching.

In *Goddesses in Everywoman*, for example, Jean Shinoda Bolen identifies the characteristics of seven well-known Greek goddesses, and how they manifest in women's personalities, attitudes, and behaviors. Her archetypes of the feminine are: **Artemis**, goddess of the hunt and the moon; **Athena,** goddess of wisdom and craft; **Hestia,** goddess of the hearth; **Hera,** goddess of marriage; **Demeter,** the Great Mother, goddess of grain; **Persephone,** abducted maiden and queen of the underworld; and **Aphrodite,** goddess of love and beauty.

Though Shinoda Bolen has written a counterpart on the male psyche, *Gods in Everyman*, the seven archetypes of the divine feminine can also be found in men, regardless of sexual orientation. Sometimes, I have a sense of which archetypes show up in a classroom or workshop just by observing the way someone is dressed. *Aphrodite's*, for example, tend to dazzle in every way, dressed boldly, often with dramatic style and sometimes displaying more flesh than many of us would be comfortable exposing. There is something captivating, alluring, about an *Aphrodite;* she tends to be the life of the gathering, the focus of everyone's attention, a source of endlessly creative ideas and the person least likely to follow through with promises and responsibilities. Then there are the *Hestia* types who tend to look as though their attire is either home-made or else pulled from the racks at Goodwill Thrift. They are the natural contemplatives who prefer staying home to partying and reading a good book to heading to the bar. Quiet and withdrawn, they have a wealth of wisdom if anyone cares to listen to them. Then there is *Persephone*— naïve, very "girly," pretty in pink with frills, flounces, and not much common sense; she is the follower and people pleaser, oblivious to the wiles of "Stranger Danger"...

As a teacher, workshop leader or spiritual guide, I find it useful to know with whom I am working. In classroom settings, I often create a quiz (or ask the students to do so), so that they can discover which archetypes are dominating their lives. This is always a popular activity, but I do have an ulterior motive. Once the students have identified their dominant archetype, I then divide them into study groups based on their findings. My reasoning behind this? When a group is comprised only of *Artemis* types (goal setters) and *Athena's* (wisdom figures) the work gets done, the students earn "A's," but their projects often lack sparkle. Similarly, if a group is comprised only of naïve *Persephone's* and romantically-obsessed *Aphrodite's*, nothing gets done whatsoever, and the students end up with poor to failing grades. When there is a balance, however, there is magic. This morning, for example, four groups in my *Professional Writing Class* at St. Xavier University, Chicago, each presented their final "business plan" with accompanying documentation, social media links and website. Each project was outstanding and, at the end of the class, one of the students actually commented on how helpful it had been to have a variety of personality types on the team.

But knowing what archetypes are present is not just for the sake of teamwork. In her effort to get the job done, *Artemis* can be ruthless, overbearing and unkind— completely unaware that she is being disrespectful to *Persephone*, critical of *Aphrodite*, and impatient with *Hera*. Or *Demeter*, as a mother figure, may be so intent on avoiding hurting people's feelings that she sacrifices quality of work to enable those who fail to perform. As teacher (or workshop leader), my awareness of such dynamics can help me guide the group in a more positive direction. Early this semester, for example, the *"Artemis"* in one group assumed leadership but made no effort to include two *Persephone's*. Only after my intervention did they end up changing their project idea to be more inclusive of everyone's interests and talents.

As coach, I also run into situations where an understanding of these archetypes can help me listen more deeply. A client may be having difficulties with a roommate and may be seeking ways of improving the situation. If the client is a *Hestia*, then a tidy, quiet environment is essential for his or her well-being and happiness; should the roommate be an *Aphrodite* (think late nights, endless drama and creative mess) then there is a basic incompatibility that must be addressed. If the client is a *Persephone* type from a quiet suburban or rural area, s/he may need coaching around personal safety in a big city environment— especially if *Aphrodite* is also present! More seriously, if a client's "ex" is an abandoned *Hera*, then jealous rage, revenge and even violence can follow. Countless stories in the news reflect this any time there are murder-suicides involving former partners and their children. An in-depth archetypal understanding of this pattern can help a coach make appropriate referrals and perhaps even save lives.

All this merely scratches the surface as to why cultivating a symbolic imagination will enhance one's abilities as a life coach. Whether a coach uses **Image Guidance** as a tool or simply becomes more mythically literate, s/he will be able to provide a richer coaching experience with more successful outcomes.

CHAPTER THREE:
DARING TO DREAM

One of the greatest privileges as a coach is to accompany a client who is on the edge of a seismic life-change. At such a moment, not only is everything in flux, but there are multiple possibilities and outcomes to consider; the only "non-option" is doing nothing. The ground shakes, the building sways, and the client is ready to take first steps away from familiar territory into something new. What the client needs is clarity, encouragement, support, as well as the time to pause and reflect. There is sometimes pain involved – a leaving behind of the old; sometimes, there is also a sense of trepidation, a fear of failure. This is where the coach is in the unique position of helping "midwife" the change that is about to take place. The coach's presence, in fact, can validate the journey and keep the client accountable to his or her own agenda of change.

Betty, a seasoned life-coach with an impressive background in law, counseling and ministry, was ready for something new. After years of putting her dreams on hold to deal with family crises, she was ready to explore options. Her agenda at the start of our coaching call was to figure out how to establish a group coaching practice and to explore what it might look like in terms of size, constituents, structure, content, and funding. While Betty had worked with support groups before, she had not consciously developed a group approach to coaching, something she had wanted to do from her first days as a new coach. I honed-in on the words, *what it might look like."*

COACH: "Well, have you looked at this practice as a visual— in other words, have you tried *picturing* it?"

There was silence—-and then an admission.

BETTY: "I've thought about components of it, but I haven't really let myself dream."

I paused, feeling the weight of those words and the sadness they communicated. I sensed that it would be impossible to move forwards with Betty's agenda without first honoring her dreaming. Imagery seemed to be the best way to do this.

COACH: "Why don't you take a few minutes to close your eyes and then describe the first thing that comes to mind. This might give us a sense of possibility"

Betty's response was immediate.

BETTY: "Well, this is funny. The first thing that comes to mind is a smile. I don't know if it's the group's smile or my smile, but it does seem as though I'm smiling at the group. It's a smile of affirmation. I can see the group taking place physically in my home office or on the phone, which is what I'm gravitating towards. Actually, coaching "remotely" offers flexibility in terms of location, but if I use the phone, I will have to become more tech savvy to manage the group. I can see it is made up of six-eight people— more like eight, perhaps. I'm imagining the duration of each meeting would be about ninety minutes. Or maybe an hour— or perhaps seventy-five minutes. Yes, I can see the group, but I've no idea what I'm talking about! Maybe that's part of the problem."

COACH: "So has the smile been consistent while you've been visualizing all this?"

BETTY: "Now I'm feeling excitement in my belly, rather than a smile. It feels energizing— there's joy and comfort! I like the idea of leading discussion without having a public face. Even though I'm working on a book, I prefer not to be center stage and don't want to be on lecture tours or giving interviews. I'm wanting to smile again!"

COACH: "If you're comfortable doing this, visualize yourself talking to the group and see if any topics come to mind— it's worth a try!"

Again, the response was immediate.

BETTY: "We're discussing something important, something that matters to me. I can imagine social/emotional intelligence groups— groups of grad students or undergrad seniors who would benefit from knowing how we communicate with each other. My vision expands beyond emerging young professionals to anyone who would benefit –women, men perhaps. Yes, especially men – they need it the most! I can see the topics evolving— topics like leadership. My focus on leadership tends to be relational and explores how to open the space to communicate. There's a smile on my face right now; I feel I can do this without moving into the unknown. This is all familiar territory— I can use my strengths and respond to what the world needs."

COACH: "So you would be taking the familiar into new territory; it's not about developing new skills?"

BETTY: "Yes. Wow…"

COACH: "I'm seeing the smile on your face and hearing the energy in your voice as you describe these groups. I'm feeling your enthusiasm. Would this be an accurate way of describing how you feel right now?"

BETTY: "Absolutely! And I do have a smile on my face right now!"

COACH: "So what is holding you back?

BETTY: "I've worked with so many who want these kinds of discussions for free, especially in a church environment. Will people spend? Will they want to join my groups?"

There was a tangible drop in energy. As Betty had enthusiastically described her sense of what the group practice could be, I found myself thinking of the "Energizer Bunny," frenetically beating its drum as each new idea surfaced. Now the Bunny was winding down, almost to a standstill.

COACH: "So the smile has gone. It's there when you talk about the group, the work, your content, but it begins to fade when you think about whether this plan is financially viable. But suppose, just suppose, it is not individuals who are your clients but some institution or organization. Then what?"

BETTY: "It's strange you should say that. I thought earlier today that perhaps I could visit my Alma Mater, Duke University, and talk to the Dean of Students about offering programming. What you're making me see right now is that I can shape programs for BlueCross and other major employers in the area. If I'm offering educational opportunities, I can see working at the corporate level. Then I won't have to worry about being paid or marketing my skills."

COACH: "When you approach the Dean of Students at Duke or the head of HR at BlueCross, how do you look? Can you visualize yourself meeting with them?"

BETTY: "I'm dressed in business casual— don't want to look too corporate. I can see I have some hesitation. The setting is not the problem— my background is corporate, after all, but I've made an intentional move away from this world to focus on people and their well-being. This is weird. It feels like I'm taking a step backwards, but this would just be a short-term comment; moreover—"

COACH: "How would this be different?"

BETTY: "In the past, I was doing regulatory work; I was also building managers. It was a good fit—so much so that I sometimes chastise myself for staying away from corporations. Will my skills be rusty now? That worries me."

COACH: "But are *these* the skills you presently have to offer? Would the institutions and corporations hire you because of your corporate background or because of something else?"

BETTY: "Well, the something else – my coaching skills, my people skills, my ability to facilitate meaningful conversations and teach communication – all of the above! Then, of course, there is my JD, my ministry background, my experience with not-for-profits, my corporate background, but I have so much more to bring to the table. What you've helped me do here is imagine beyond what I'd been thinking. The imagery has helped expand the vision. I feel myself still smiling."

COACH: "Well, you're extraordinarily well-qualified to do so much, but it's your energy and wisdom that are going to carry you forwards, not all the degrees and certificates."

BETTY: "I don't want to help people simply make money, but to change the world. I'm at my best when ministry and coaching come together. I help clients dig deep and get things done, working from the inside out. That's when I shine – not 'shiny' as in arrogance but a feeling of aliveness, a sense of being, an experience of flow. Through these groups, I would be offering not just educational opportunities but the gift of life."

COACH: "This is very profound– a gift for the universe! The challenge, of course, will be how to tend the flame and keep the flow going once we hang up the phone. On a practical level, what I've heard in the last twenty minutes or so is that you've come up with a concept for the group, the number of groups, the content of the groups, the number of participants, the means of delivering the experience and ways of securing funding. Is the smile still there?"

BETTY: "Yes, it's now a smile with a forward-looking agenda. This is great!"

COACH: "So what's your plan of action, the 'next steps?'"

BETTY: "The first thing is to develop content, to understand what's currently being offered, what is needed and what I can offer to meet that need. Maybe I should form a test-group to develop procedures. I need to think about the content in such a way that I can discuss it intelligently. It shouldn't take much time to sketch out the content for two or three groups— perhaps a month. I won't fully develop content until I receive a 'go ahead' for each group. I will reach out to places where I still have strong contacts– Duke, my old workplace…"

COACH: "This sounds good. If you had said six months, I would have been concerned about losing impetus. This may be a little premature but what steps lie beyond this?"

BETTY: "Perhaps I need to leverage the book I'm working on."

COACH: "I know you've said in the past that you feel detached from this book, but suppose it's a piece of the next step and simply needs to be reshaped? As a writer myself, I know how deadly it can be to work on a book if you don't have a sense of passion."

BETTY: "Funny you say this. I was thinking just today how I've targeted the book to individual coachees when I could also target the work place."

COACH: "Which means the smile is now extended to the book."

BETTY: "Right."

COACH *(laughing):* "So it's a big smile, Betty!"

BETTY: "Lots of food for thought, that's for sure."

If I look back on this coaching conversation, I am struck by the way Betty's image of a smile guided both of us in our interactions. By asking Betty if she could picture her practice, I was taking a risk. Betty, of course, could have brushed off my suggestion or could have simply said, *"I don't want to go there."* Instead, her willingness to enter the world of the imagination allowed the imagination to speak to her. The smile came as confirmation that her plans for developing her coaching practice were in sync with her core desires, values and skills. She experienced "excitement in my [her] belly," as well as joy and comfort; the clearer her plans became, the more heightened her feelings. In fact, I was feeling her energy and excitement over the telephone and this, in turn, sharpened my ability as a coach to respond, affirm, challenge and pose questions. I, too, entered her imaginative world, seeing what Betty saw and sharing in her feelings of elation.

When her energy dipped and feelings of doubt surfaced, I was aware of that as well; I felt myself become disappointed for her but was still able to offer a suggestion regarding funding that opened up new possibilities for forming corporate and academic partnerships. I empathized deeply but still functioned with enough objectivity to help move Betty's agenda forwards. I would say that my coaching presence was at its best because the two of us were at a place of At-One-Ment.

BJM's Response:

It's funny. As a coach, I often ask clients questions like, "What does that look like," or "Can you imagine what life will be like when you reach this goal?" Using such visualization, I try to help clients get clarity on their current circumstances and their goals. I did not know that, in a way, I was doing image guidance. Nor have I had others so adeptly guide me through this process. I love how Liz followed my energy and challenged me to go deeper. Sticking with the image of my smile for an extended period greatly expanded my creative thinking. Who knew the riches that could be found behind a simple smile once it was noticed and explored?

CHAPTER FOUR:
IMAGE GUIDANCE & DISCERNMENT

In coaching, the term "decision-making" is probably more commonly used than "discernment." Though the two terms might be considered roughly synonymous, I believe there is a difference between the two. "Decision-making" involves weighing the facts, looking at options, imagining outcomes, checking in with one's deepest desires and then taking the next step. All of the above is included in the discernment process, but there are additional factors to consider. While decision-making involves being fully informed so that one can make the best choice possible, discernment also includes a spiritual dimension. For some clients, this can be articulated in religious language as *"God's will"*; others may be more comfortable asking, *"What does the universe need of me?"* or *"Where am I being called?"* or *"What is my unique mission in life that no one else can accomplish?"* or *"How can I live a more purposeful life?"*

Such questions cannot be answered by facts alone; often, clients look within for their answers, turning to their higher power or to the universe to guide them. As I state in *Image Guidance: A Tool for Spiritual Direction*, "chance conversations, intuitive hunches, symbolic happenings, dreams, moments of awareness and sometimes even "signs" can alert us as to what might be the most life-giving decision (71). **Image Guidance** can also help the client get to the heart of the matter:

> **Image Guidance** is an effective tool in the discernment process because it puts us in touch with our deepest feelings while raising possibilities that we might otherwise not have dared imagine. At the same time, it doesn't

replace the more conventional tasks of observing and listening, but it supplements what we learn and, in some cases, takes us further in our investigations: we not only have the full benefit of our rational selves and of others' thoughtful input; we also draw on the world of the unconscious, tapping its resources in surprising and dramatic ways (74).

Discernment, then, goes beyond a cerebral activity. It involves the whole self, as well as deep listening to the call of the universe. As a process, it honors transitions as a sacred time that can lead to a more fulfilling life. The outcomes it seeks have to do with mission, vision and personal fulfillment, rather than income, status, success and other external measures of worth. At the time of this writing, Ola, an international student from Poland, is in transition. About to graduate from Columbia College, Chicago, with a B.A. in Photography, she would love to visit her family whom she has not seen in five years; however, there is a possibility that she would not be allowed back in the United States on her student visa. She is hoping to extend her visa by a year so that she can pay off her student loan of close to $20,000 before returning to Europe, but there are no guarantees that she will receive the extension or find a job here.

Moreover, when the idea originally surfaced about staying for the extra year, she had assumed her parents would be coming to the States for her graduation. As it turns out, they will be unable to get the necessary visas, and so if she doesn't visit them, it will have been more than six years before they see each other again. She not only misses her family but is concerned about their growing older and the possibility of "something happening" to them before she can return. These emotions run deep and have been heightened by her father's recent expression of how much he misses her. Coming from a man who doesn't openly talk about his feelings, this has made Ola aware of how her choices have impacted her loved ones as well as herself.

To complicate matters, Ola doesn't wish to live in Poland and, were she forced to return there, it would take her ten years or more to repay the student loan, given typical salary ranges. Her family, meanwhile, is looking forward to her visit, but her legal advisors are warning her against leaving the country. Right now, she enjoys a wonderful living arrangement with a host family that has provided food, shelter, salary and financial assistance in return for childcare; while continuing to be supportive, the family needs to know her plans as they will need to hire a nanny to replace her, should she decide to leave the States.

When we met, Ola's agenda was to explore "next steps" or find alternative solutions that she had not yet considered. She expressed gratitude for the fact that she had been able to fulfill her academic dreams but was also aware that she has paid a heavy price for "following her bliss." Since her situation was so complicated, we agreed that we would try using **Image Guidance** as a tool in our coaching session; I invited her to close her eyes.

COACH: "Ola, what image comes to mind when you think about paying the price?"

OLA: "I see a bright golden coin, a clean coin. Some coins are dark, but this one shines, spinning, showing off. I see an eagle on it – there's a coin in Poland with an eagle…."

COACH: "A gold coin?"

OLA: "No, the Polish coin is a silver one."

COACH: "Okay. When you see the gold coin spinning, how do you feel?"

OLA: "Something comes to me that money plays a role in my world, that it has played a role in my fate, even an unwanted role. It's almost a stigma I carry that I grew up without money and that made me driven. I was the only person I could rely on; there was no one else to count on. I was always independent and driven. I always had to be top of my class, so I could achieve something and be someone, and not have to face the struggles my parents faced. Education would be my ticket to the future. Even as a child, I thought that if I'm smart, I'd be able to help both my parents and me. I wanted to take my parents places – for example, to the coast of France."

COACH: "So how would you define this coin?"

OLA: "It reflects my relationship with money which is a helpful tool – nice to have but right now my need for it is slowing me down, even if I decide not to stay here. I just want to pay off my debt and support my parents, so they can leave their jobs and have some financial stability. But I don't want to get caught up in the rat race; that's not for me. Once the debt is paid off, that's the last time I want to worry about money. I don't think I'll need a lot— just enough for food and a small house. So long as I can do something I enjoy; I'm a free spirit, and I don't want to get a job simply to make money."

COACH: "This may sound a little silly, but what questions would you like to ask the coin?"

OLA: "I want to ask if one day I will actually take my parents places and give them a more secure retirement. I had an aunt who could read palms; I remember her taking my hand and telling me I had the potential to make money and be wealthy. I really want to believe her."

COACH: "Ola, if you're comfortable doing this, try asking the coin directly and see what happens."

OLA: "I ask the questions, but there's no clear answer. I only see the golden glow of the coin which I like."

COACH: "What else can you see?"

OLA: "I see the golden glow blending in with a calm, peaceful white light. If I believed in heaven, that is probably what it would look like."

COACH: "This sounds very positive— the light shows that your intentions are good and loving. There is nothing materialistic or selfish about your dreams. The possibility of making money is there, but what else are you hearing?"

OLA: "I'm not hearing anything. There are no words, but I see the image of a hot air balloon, with a lot of people. Travel. I'm not sure what it's telling me, but if you were to ask me what I want to do, I would say I'm ready to leave… I want to go. I'm not sure that staying another year in America would make a difference, but this may be my intellect speaking … logic."

COACH: "What is really important is that you're saying you would leave if you didn't have this debt. What would happen if you returned to Poland after graduation?"

OLA: "I feel fear in my gut. It would be wonderful to go back to see my parents, to go to the forest, but I don't think I would know what to do if I lived there. There is no challenge or excitement there for me. It feels dark like a closed chapter. I would make it work if I had to, but I don't want to go back… just visit. It's difficult to think I can't go home. With a few clicks on my computer, I could go home tomorrow. But the extra year in Chicago would give me the way to pay off my debt. If I had a secure job or internship, I would stay here and delay my visit. Then I could relocate somewhere other than Poland."

COACH: "That's interesting! What countries would you consider?"

OLA: "The language and traditions of soul in Central and South America speak to me. There's color and energy, a closeness to spirituality. I have the same feelings about Africa. I would be super-excited to immerse myself in another linguistic world and to meet new people. But I would not be able to pay off my debt, if I lived there. The salaries would be too low."

COACH: "So what would it be like if you couldn't come back?"

OLA: "It wouldn't be the end of the world. I feel clarity coming to my body, into my soul. I feel if it's meant to be, I can come back and if not, I'll stay there or relocate to another country. It's only money. I'm not cutting off a limb or anything like that."

COACH: "What other possibilities do you see?"

OLA: "There *are* options – I have contacts with a Safari Company in South Africa where perhaps I could be a photographer. Here, in Chicago, I have a beautiful basement apartment, with a lot of space, food on the table, an easy job, a lovely neighborhood, and I'm treated as one of the family; I have a weekly income, and this is how I would pay off my debt. But I'm twenty-seven and have the urge to be independent and not live under someone else's roof."

COACH: "What would be another option?"

OLA: "When I was focusing on the gold coin, I also saw a ship surrounded by a lot of water—a cruise ship. There are a lot of people. It's a happy image, but I don't see myself in the picture. Reminds me of the image of the hot air balloon. Perhaps I could be a photographer on a cruise ship. I know this would just be a job and that photography as an art form would be lost. I'm not sure that I would be treated like a whole person or even respected. I would just be snapping pictures of wealthy people rather than creating art."

COACH: "What would it be like to do this for a year?"

OLA: "I could do it—I could totally do it! In my mind, I see a lot of travel, but the exploration would be exciting. I love Chicago but if you're stuck in one place…. I like this idea of moving a lot, of tasting a little of this and switching back to that and finding what my favorite flavor is."

Shortly after our session, Ola sent me a copy of the letter of application she was sending to a cruise company, along with links to her Portfolio, website and Instagram account. She had come in to see me with a complex situation which was full of *"What if's?" What if she stayed in Chicago an extra year— what might happen to her parents? What if she went to visit them after graduating and wasn't allowed back in the United States? What if she did stay in Chicago but her new job or internship would not provide the flexible hours she needed to work for her host family? What if she moved back to Poland for a few years? What if she moved to Central or South America or perhaps to Africa?*

Addressing these concerns through a "regular" coaching conversation would not have got us very far, because everything was uncertain. Without knowing the various outcomes of her range of possible decisions, it was difficult to untangle "best options." The image that came to me was of long strands of cooked spaghetti that needed to be pried apart. The use of **Image Guidance**, however, allowed for a playful exploration of fears, feelings, dreams, values, and possibilities. The Gold Coin allowed Ola to articulate what would be life-giving for her and what would be "death-dealing" in a metaphorical sense. What emerged most clearly was that Ola wanted to protect both the artist within and her spiritual path; her vision was long-term and had to do with the kind of life she wanted to live, far away from "the rat race." While she intended to fulfill her financial and family responsibilities, she was not ready to sacrifice herself for the sake of money or success. The emerging short-term plan was to leave Chicago, visit her family in Poland and then work as a photographer to pay off her student loan –perhaps in a Safari Park or on a cruise ship. After that, the world would be hers, on her terms.

Although in the previous case study Ola had come in with a discernment-based agenda, there are times when the client is unaware that discernment is the *real* agenda that needs to be addressed. Recently, a couple made an appointment for marriage coaching; their stated agenda was to work on communication skills, but while I was watching their interactions, I became aware of a negative energy field emanating from the husband. I could l feel his repressed anger from across the room. I also noted that whenever he spoke to me about his wife, in front of her, he referred to her as "she" and not by name. For her part, the wife seemed defensive and accusatory. As I picked up visuals, tone of voice and my own physical reactions to the conversation, I could see that both were trying to protect their own professional turf from each other; both wanted to take their careers to the next level but felt held back in terms of their marriage and because of their responsibilities for their infant, a month-old baby girl.

"Hilda" had taken maternity leave but was now ready to return to her law firm where she was a rising star. "Hugo" was in medical school but had yet to decide upon a specialty; his wife was pressuring him to consider dermatology or ophthalmology because she reasoned that these specialties would be less demanding than others and would allow him more time at home to help raise their child. Our session began something like this:

COACH: "In your *Welcome Package*, you expressed the desire to focus on building communication skills. Could you share with me why this would be important for you right now?"

HUGO: "Yeah… she's always nagging me. Every time we interact, she's pointing out something I've failed to do, like take my shoes off when I come through the door, or recycle plastic bottles. She'll even send me texts at work letting me know when I've left dishes in the sink or laundry on the floor. It's like she's deliberately trying to needle me."

COACH: "And what do those needles feel like?"

HUGO: "Needles, of course. Like sharp needles that puncture me all over."

COACH: "And when you feel these needles puncture you, what happens?"

HUGO: "Well, then I'll send her a text back, reminding her about the wet clothes still in the dryer or how her hair is clogging the bathroom sink."

COACH: "So what I'm hearing is that you send her needles back. Hilda, when you remind Hugo about household chores, he feels you are attacking him. How does this make *you* feel?"

HILDA: "Shitty. I don't mean to nag him, but we agreed on household rules which were important to us –like not wearing street shoes in the house, keeping the place tidy and recycling when possible. The two of us came up with the rules, but I'm the only one keeping them."

COACH: "And when you hear Hugo saying that you 'needle' him, what's your reaction?"

HILDA: "That's pretty strong language. I don't intend to hurt him, but sometimes it's the only way I can get through to him."

COACH: "What I'm hearing is that you then puncture his complacency with sharp messages. What might you do differently?"

HILDA: "I'd be willing to stop what he calls 'nagging' if he stops being angry all the time."

COACH: "And how do you know he's angry?"

HILDA: "He looks like he looks now – uptight, doesn't smile, ignores me, pushes me away, refuses to talk…."

COACH: "Hugo, what's your response to what Hilda has just said?"

HUGO: "Well, I'm not angry with *her*."

COACH: "Can you say more about this?"

HUGO: "I'm just angry with life. I feel I'm being dragged in a direction I don't want to go."

COACH: "And what is dragging you?"

HUGO: "I don't know. Life, I guess."

COACH: "Let's stop here for a minute. I'm going to ask you to close your eyes and to visualize whatever is dragging you along. When you can see something, let me know, but keep your eyes closed."

HUGO: "Okay. What I'm seeing is a ball and chain around my ankles – you know, the kind convicts wear. I can't see what's dragging me, but something is pulling me by the ball and chain."

COACH: "And how do you look in this picture?"

HUGO: "Terrified. I feel I've been sentenced to death or perhaps life imprisonment."

COACH: "If you're comfortable doing this, ask the ball and chain why they are wrapped around your ankles."

HUGO: "This sounds silly—and I've opened my eyes now—but I heard that the ball and chain will be my fate if I make the wrong choice."

COACH: "And what would that be?"

HUGO: "I've no interest in dermatology and even less in ophthalmology; what I really want to do is orthopedic surgery, but there's a five- year residency and long hours, so it won't exactly fit in with family life."

During the rest of the session, we processed Hugo's desire to become an orthopedic surgeon and the impact this would have on their marriage and family life. Hilda conceded she had been selfish for insisting that her husband select a specialty that was based on convenience rather than on what would give him a sense of fulfillment.

The ball and chain image brought home her husband's sense of frustration and hopelessness; she now understood that he had been projecting his anger on to her since she was the one who had pushed for dermatology or ophthalmology. As for Hugo, the more he talked about the possibility of studying orthopedics, the more he became animated. The negative energy field that I had picked up soon faded, and he became visibly more relaxed. At the point where he spontaneously took Hilda's hand in his and squeezed it, we began to examine their typical patterns of communication. Our agenda for the next session would be how both parents could balance their careers with marriage and having children.

NOTE:

Before going to press, I received a text message from an elated Ola: she has just been offered the position of Portrait Artist on a cruise line and intends to accept. So wonderful to know she is on her way!

CHAPTER FIVE:
COACHING WITH RELIGIOUS IMAGERY

If one's coaching practice is explicitly spiritual, whether generically so or whether affiliated with a specific faith tradition, then the coach can expect religious imagery to surface; moreover, the coach is most likely comfortable with that imagery, especially if he or she comes from a similar faith background to the client. Even if there is a difference in faith traditions, a coach from a religious background is usually able to interpret symbolism from an archetypal perspective. Images of water, for example, generally suggest cleansing, as in the sacred rivers of Hinduism, or the washing rituals before Muslim prayer, or the waters of Baptism in Christianity; similarly, images of mountain peaks often communicate a sense of transcendence while desert imagery typically signifies spiritual aridity.

In the case of mythical content, the literal level of the symbolism may not be "true" historically, but it is "real" on a spiritual level. Take, for example, the *Journey of the Magi* in the infancy narratives of Jesus (Mt 2:1-12). This narrative could either be taken to be literally/historically true or could be interpreted to represent the universal significance of the birth of the Christ Child— or both. Does it matter whether there were three, six or zero Magi or Kings? What is important is the symbolic significance of their recognizing the Christ – an Epiphany for the Gentiles. The mythical pattern represented here is that of the spiritual quest: The Magi leave the comfort and safety of home to follow a star; they risk everything for the sake of this star; they give themselves completely to the journey; as a result, they undergo a transformation of consciousness, returning home as "missionaries."

This pattern is also the classic *Heroic Quest*. Other mythical patterns to be found in sacred stories include but are not limited to the *Saving of The Wasteland* (Arthurian Legends); the *Night Sea Journey* (Jonah, Pinocchio); *Creation Myths* (versions can be found in every culture); the *Quest for Immortality* (*Epic of Gilgamesh*); *Myths of Fall* (Adam and Eve); *Myths of Resurrection* (Osiris, Dionysius, Jesus) and so forth....

To know the symbol system of one faith tradition often provides the key to understanding the symbols of another tradition— not with 100 % accuracy, perhaps, but with enough fluency to get the "gist" of what the imagery is communicating. Most, if not all, religious symbols seem to originate in what C.G. Jung named "the collective unconscious," that is, in the level of the psyche common to all humanity. While the "personal unconscious" is made up of our own memories, dreams, and reflections, according to Jung, the "collective unconscious" is of a "collective, universal and impersonal nature which is identical in all individuals"; in other words, the collective unconscious contains the shared memories of the whole human race (60). Here, the archetypal content of myths and dreams takes form, providing humanity with a common symbolic language.

The advantage for the spiritual coach in dealing with religious imagery is that the client is not only comfortable with such imagery but *expects* it to be present. The client, in fact, has contracted to work with this coach because he or she wants a spiritual focus in coaching. This creates a "win-win" situation in which both coach and client are in their comfort zones. Though there is always the danger that the coach might assume an image means one thing while the client understands something entirely different, for the most part, with the aid of clarifying questions, the spiritual coach can take advantage of the religious imagery to help move the client's agenda forwards. Difficulties surface, however, if the coach is unfamiliar with the client's symbol system and has no idea how to relate to it. This is more likely to happen in life coaching that is secular; however, there may be times when even the spiritual coach feels challenged. The options are either to avoid exploring the imagery (not recommended); or to have the client explain what he or she understands by the imagery (a better option); or to develop one's own religious literacy (best option). A course in world religions based on primary texts from the world's great religious traditions would be a starting point, as would a course in mythology. Of course, one can begin a self-study program, but that requires much discipline and knowing which texts to read in the first place, as well as understanding how to interpret them.

What makes it worthwhile for any coach to be comfortable with religious imagery is that it allows us to take the client to a deeper place. Drawing on the work of Jean Houston and Robert Masters, Ewert Cousins describes four levels to the psyche:

1) The *Sensorium*, or the level of heightened sense experience;

2) The *Ontogenetic*, or recollective analytical level, where the subject recalls his or her personal history. This level corresponds to Freudian psychoanalysis;

3) The *Phylogenetic* or symbolic level, corresponding to the collective unconscious of Jung. Here the subject relives the great myths and rituals of humankind;

4) The level of integral consciousness, or the *Mysterium.* This is the level of deep mystical consciousness, which is similar to that described by the mystics of the world. (35)

I would venture to say that most coaching happens at the level of the *ontogenetic*, or the level of personal history. Unlike therapy, coaching is forward-focused rather than historical, but it does involve personal narrative. The initial forming of an agenda often has roots in past experiences and events such as an executive being fired or having to face unsuccessful patterns of workplace leadership or wanting to create a more fulfilling role within the corporation. There is also a historical component in the case of a couple seeking relationship coaching; without remembering what brought them together in the first place, they lose the "magic" that will keep them together in the future. I am not suggesting that the coach adopt a Freudian approach to the past, but most clients can only move forward by addressing what "happened" yesterday. Even the value of exploring what has "happened" between coaching sessions involves an *ontogenetic* component. There is no question that historical narrative of a reflective, non-therapeutic nature has a definite place in life coaching.

A coach who is skilled in mindfulness and meditation may also work with the client at the level of the *sensorium*. There can be an explicit agreement between client and coach that these elements will form part of the coaching agenda; however, even without such an agreement, the coach can work at this level. Simply asking the question, *"How does this make you feel?"* takes the client to the *sensorium*. Expand the question to, *"Where in your body are your feeling this emotion?"* and the client is further immersed in sensory reality. Anyone who has ever asked such questions will understand the value of doing so: The client is immediately taken out of *cerebral* understanding into *somatic* understanding. The mind might struggle to understand what the body already knows. When we feel fear in our gut or can name that grief has fractured our hearts, then we step away from self-analysis into the experience we may have repressed. That would allow a coach to help us face our situation more fully, thus empowering us to move into a new reality. When all our senses are engaged in interpreting our unique situation, then we have a wealth of knowledge that will take us far beyond anything our minds can conjure up.

This brings us to the *phylogenetic* level. Here, symbols manifest that are universal in nature, taking us beyond our personal symbols and experiences, into unknown territory; here, the customary laws of time and space seem to break down, and we may have flashbacks to events that happened decades –even centuries or millennia—before we were born. Two stories stand out which illustrate this. I remember a student's surprise when I led a meditation session based on the letters of the Hebrew Alphabet. It turned out that she'd had a reoccurring dream in which she saw an unfamiliar symbol; not knowing what it was, she drew the image and then had it "inked" onto her arm. The symbol in question was the letter *shin,* the letter that begins the word *"shalom"* and *"Shabbat."* The discovery that this was one of the most sacred letters in the Hebrew Alphabet impressed her greatly, as she had experienced its power each time it appeared in her dreams – hence the tattoo!

The second story is based on a burial ritual. Many years ago, a friend of mine—a Catholic priest— had journeyed to Ireland to bury his teenage cousin. The young man had been sniffing glue with his classmates, but while they merely got "high," he died from the experience. At the gravesite, after all the traditional rites and prayers, his classmates spontaneously began throwing personal items into the grave— soccer jerseys, rings, scarves, coins… My friend later learned that the pre-Christian Celts had buried their dead with food, clothing, money, chariots and anything else they might have needed in the afterlife. Without knowing this, to honor their fallen comrade, the grieving students had performed a burial ritual that was thousands of years old.

If, as coaches, we are comfortable at the *phylogenetic* level of consciousness, we will be able to ask powerful questions that address the symbolic or mythical dimension of the client's experience. Instead of ignoring the imagery, we can invite the client to stay with it. The client, for example, might complain that his direct reports expect him to be a "savior" figure. The coach then might respond in a variety of ways: *"What do you understand by a savior?"; "What is it about saviors that you find burdensome?"; "What does it feel like to be the department 'savior'?"; "What qualities or behaviors might encourage your reports to view you as their savior?"; "What would be a healthier role for you in the department?"; "What stories have shaped your understanding of what it means to be a savior?"* Simply by focusing on the word "savior," the coach can facilitate a conversation in which the client begins to recognize his tendency to play the "savior" and why this might not be helpful either to him or to his team; the client may then become more open to looking at alternative forms of leadership that leave everyone feeling empowered.

Another client might claim that she is being "crucified" by her co-workers. To by-pass this extreme language without further exploration is to miss the deepest dimensions of her experience. The coach could ask, *"What do you understand by being crucified?"; "What aspects of Jesus' crucifixion fit your experience?"; "Who is doing the crucifying?"; "What effect is this having on you"* and *"Is there anything you can do to get off this cross?"* As an outcome of these questions, the client might articulate that, through no fault of her own, her colleagues are treating her with great cruelty and that their attacks are negatively affecting her emotions and physical health. Further conversation might reveal that the client sees herself as the innocent victim whereas, in fact, some of her actions or attitudes may be at the root of her colleagues' alleged cruelty towards her; moreover, as powerful questions lead to greater clarity, it may become apparent that what she is interpreting as "cruel" behaviors may be nothing more than her colleagues trying to question her decisions or provide constructive feedback. It may turn out that the client has been "crucifying" herself!

Just as a dream dictionary offers a limited approach to dream interpretation, so a "symbol dictionary" would be similarly limited as a coaching resource. Each symbol, after all, not only has its universal dimension but also its *personal* dimension, a reality that dictionaries cannot accommodate. Nevertheless, compiling a list of the types of religious symbols that tend to reoccur in coaching contexts could be useful. Looking back at the religious imagery I have encountered in both life coaching and spiritual direction, I would add the following randomly-selected biblical symbols to such a list; please note that to compile a comprehensive list of biblical symbols or to include the primary symbols of other faith traditions lies way behind the scope of this book:

The Garden   The place of innocence and beauty from where sinners are banished (Gn 3)

The Snake or   The Tempter/ Great Deceiver (Gn 3)

Serpent

Forbidden Fruit	Forbidden object of desire (Gn 3)
Cain	First son of Adam and Eve who murders his brother Abel (Gn 4)
The Flood	Waters of destruction that destroy humankind on account of their wickedness (Gn 6-8)
Noah's Ark	A place of safety for the "righteous few" in times of danger and destruction such as the Flood (Gn 6-8)
40 Days/Nights	Sacred number 40: it rains for 40 days and 40 nights when Noah and his family are in the ark; the Hebrew people wander in the desert for 40 years; Jesus fasts in the desert for 40 days etc.
Rainbow	Sign of the covenant between God, humanity and all creatures (Gn 9:12-17)
Tower of Babel	Humanity attempts to create a towering civilization without God, and so God confuses human efforts by creating a diversity of languages (Gn 11:1-9)
Sodom/Gomorrah	Towns with evil inhabitants that bring death and destruction on themselves by refusing to repent (Gn 19:1-29)
Pillar of Salt	Lot's wife turns into a pillar of salt when she looks back on the destruction of Sodom and Gomorrah (Gn 19:26)

Sacrifice of Isaac	Abraham's willingness to obey God and kill his only son proves his faith and leads to Isaac's last-minute deliverance (Gn 22)
Pharaoh	Oppressive ruler (Ex 1-14)
Burning Bush	Place of awe, fear and trembling where the presence of the Holy One is manifest (Ex 2:23-25)
10 Plagues	God sends ten plagues to punish Pharaoh when he refuses to let God's people go (Ex 7-11)
Parting Waters	Reference to Moses splitting the Sea of Reeds so the Hebrews can pass to the other side on dry ground (Ex 14:10-31)
Manna	Miraculous food that appears on a daily basis as the Hebrew people wander in the desert for 40 years (Ex 16)
Golden Calf	Object of idolatry (Ex 32)
Promised Land	The ultimate destination, a God-given place of new beginnings and possibilities (Gn 15:18-21)
Land/Milk/Honey	Another reference to the Promised Land
David & Goliath	Young David kills the giant Goliath with just a pebble and a slingshot (1 Sam 17:41-51)
Job	A righteous, prosperous chieftain who loses everything but remains faithful to God; he

learns to see God as a result of his sufferings (Book of Job)

Dry Bones   Ezekiel's vision of a Valley of Dry Bones. Here everyone has lost life and spirit; only God can restore the walking dead to life (Ezk 37)

Belly of the Fish   Running from God and from his mission to the people of Nineveh, Jonah is swallowed by the Great Fish. There he remains for three days and three nights, as if in the tomb, and experiences conversion (Jonah 2)

The Star   The heavenly sign announcing the birth of the King of Kings (Mt 2:1-12)

Magi   The astronomers who follow the star in search of the newborn king (Mt 2:1-12)

Herod   The wicked king who tries to destroy the Christ Child (Mt 2: 13-15)

Light   "You are the light of the world. A city set on a mountain cannot be hidden. Nor do they light a lamp and then put it under a bushel basket" (Mt 5:14-16)

Pearls & Swine   "Do not give what is holy to dogs, or throw your pearls before swine" (Mt 7:6)

Weeds & Wheat   Weeds co-exist with wheat until harvest when weeds will be burned, and the wheat will be gathered into the barn (Mt 13:24-30)

Nazareth	Jesus' hometown where he is rejected (Mt 14:54-58)
Walking on Water	Jesus' ability to have power over the waters and do the impossible (Mt 14:22-33)
Camel & Needle	"It is easier for a camel to pass through the eye of a needle than for one who is rich to enter the Kingdom of God" (Mt 19:24)
"Render to Caesar"	"Then give to Caesar what belongs to Caesar and to God what belongs to God" (Mt 2:21)
5 Foolish Virgins	The five wise virgins have enough oil for their lamps while the five foolish virgins do not and are therefore locked out of the wedding feast (Mt 25:1-13)
Buried Talent	Symbol of sloth and lack of spiritual fertility; the buried talent yields nothing (Mt 25:14-30)
Judas	The apostle who betrays Jesus, selling him for 30 pieces of silver (Mt 26:20-25)
Lost Sheep	"Rejoice with me because I have found my lost sheep" (Lk 15:1-7)
Prodigal Son	"Your brother was dead and has come back to life again; he was lost and has been found" (Lk 15:1-32)
Water into Wine	Jesus turns water into wine at the wedding feast at Cana (Jn 2:1-12)

Widow's Mite	"She from her poverty has offered her whole livelihood" (Lk 21:1-4)
Good Samaritan	The stranger who saves his neighbor – a Jew and therefore his "enemy"— when a priest and Levite leave him bleeding at the side of the road (Lk10:29-37)

The references given above surface with regularity in the utterances of those familiar with the bible; precisely because such references are so much a part of everyday speech, it is easy for the coach to ignore them. However, when the coach pays attention to such images, they can lead to increased awareness and understanding. For example, in response to the question, *"How are you feeling today?"* a client might answer: *"I feel rather like Job"* (implying multiple losses on every level); or *"My **star** has begun to dim"* (implying a loss of vision and sense of mission); or *"I feel like one of the **dry bones** in the Valley of Dry Bones"* (implying a lack of fertility, creativity or spiritual connectedness); or *"I realize I'm the **Lost Sheep** that still needs to be found"* (implying a sense of being existentially adrift).

The coach might also ask, *"What have you learned since our last session?"* Again, there may be a biblical flavor to the responses: *"I must stop casting my **pearls before swine**"* (implying that the client has been revealing too much to those who lack the capacity to understand, let alone respect, what has been shared); or *"I have to watch my back when there may be a **Judas** around"* (implying that the client suspects there could be a betrayer close by); or *"I realize now that I can neither **walk on water** nor **turn water into wine**"* (implying that the client once felt invincible and in control of everything, including the elements); or *"I have to face the fact that I've **buried my one and only talent**"* (implying that the client recognizes that he or she has failed to use innate gifts in a way that is productive); *"If I keep looking back, I'll be turned into a **pillar of salt**"* (implying that the client will be destroyed by the habit of constantly looking back at the past instead of building for the future).

And if the coach were to ask, as coaches do, *"What is the next step?"* the client might answer: *"I need to head towards the **Promised Land**"* (implying that the client, having settled for a place or situation that is less than healthy, is now willing to seek happiness, prosperity and fulfilment); or *"I must build myself an **ark**"* (implying the client needs to create a haven, a place the storms of life cannot destroy); *"I have to believe there is a **rainbow** somewhere on the horizon"* (implying that the client has given into negative thinking but is now ready to be more hopeful); or *"I have to make sure I have **enough oil** for my lamp"* (implying that the client needs to secure more spiritual or material resources); or *"I need to find the right pebble to topple **Goliath**"* (implying that the client is willing to take on a formidable opponent with inner power as opposed to mere weaponry).

Once the coach understands the client's religious imagery, he or she can probe further. Let's take the statement, *"I feel rather like **Job**";* here is a possible interaction between coach and client:

COACH: "So how does Job feel?"

CLIENT: "Well, you know, Job lost everything."

COACH: "That only tells me what *happened* to him."

[PAUSE]

COACH: "If you're comfortable doing this, close your eyes for a moment and try to connect with Job's feelings."

CLIENT: "*Devastated. Shunned. Worthless.* I mean, he's just lost his entire family, all his livestock, all his wealth and there he is sitting on a dung heap, covered in boils while his so-called friends say that this is all a punishment for his sins."

COACH: "You use three adjectives – 'devastated,' 'shunned,' and 'worthless.' Which one is closest to your experience?"

CLIENT: "All three actually. Look, I've lost my job; I got a raw deal in the divorce and lost the house, custody of the kids and even the dog; and, on top of all this, I now have hideous blotches all over my face."

COACH: "What might make you feel better?"

CLIENT: "I want to know, *'Why ME?'* I've made a few mistakes along the way but nothing heinous enough to deserve all this suffering."

COACH: "Let's go back to Job. I invite you to close your eyes again, and ask him if he learned anything from his experience."

CLIENT: *"Ask Job?"*

COACH: "Yes. I know this sounds a little silly, but sometimes images have wisdom to share."

[PAUSE]

CLIENT: "All I hear is, *'Bad things do happen to good people.'*"

COACH: "And what do you understand by this?"

CLIENT: "Well, this is a bit of a stretch, but I think it means that no one is exempt from suffering."

COACH: "Yeah, that would be how I interpret this as well, but I would also look at how the Bible story ends."

CLIENT: "Remind me!"

COACH: "I can't give you the exact scriptural reference or even quote the lines properly, but I believe Job says something like this: 'Before, I had heard of God by word of mouth, but now, because of my sufferings, I have seen God with my own eyes.'"

CLIENT: "That's pretty powerful!"

COACH: "Agreed, so what's the 'take-away'?"

CLIENT: "I need to stop complaining and see if there's some gift in this experience of loss. I think I can let go of the *'Why me?'*"

COACH: "That's a great first step!"

In this brief exchange with the coach, the client is not only able to express identification with Job, the classic archetype of suffering, but also to articulate the cry, *"Why me?"*; the client then moves from being a confused victim to becoming an accepting spiritual seeker. Neither the coach nor the client in this exchange has an in-depth knowledge of the *Book of Job,* but they are familiar enough with Job's story that they can see how the character of Job holds symbolic meaning that can clarify the client's predicament.

Because of the brevity of **Image Guidance** interventions in coaching contexts, it is rare that the coaching client will experience the fourth level of consciousness, the *mysterium.* Typically, it is only after extensive breathing exercises and a deep focusing on the image at hand that the client will enter a state of mystical consciousness; that is, a total leaving behind of ordinary consciousness while experiencing oneness with God, self and all beings. In this union, the client may have feelings of awe and intense intimacy with God; he or she may tune out the external world and focus only on the inner world, incapable of speech and, sometimes, even of movement. The experience may last a few minutes or extend an hour or more! Time stops— at least, chronological time no longer has relevance, for the client is caught up in Kairos, that "undetermined time in which something special happens." The coach becomes irrelevant, and any attempt to bring the client back to ordinary consciousness may seem like an intrusion.

In extended **Image Guidance** sessions, it is quite common for clients to enter the *mysterium,* but this is a "by-product," not a goal, of the process. The coach needs to be aware, however, that clients who are deeply spiritual may enter the *mysterium* quite quickly—even immediately. Images of light, fire, water, and Communion can often trigger altered states of consciousness, as in the following example adapted from ***Image Guidance: A Tool for Spiritual Direction:***

COACH: "You mentioned having a feeling of freedom. Do any images come to mind?"

CLIENT: "Yes … I see open hands outstretched, open in trust and surrender. And there's fire, flames burning …"

COACH: "Sarah, can you say anything more about the fire?"

CLIENT: "The hands are still there… the fire is all around them… swirling reds, oranges and pinks… now white steam, a fusion of sorts… it's difficult to speak…"

As Sarah sat in the stillness, I had a tangible sense of immersion in the Presence she was experiencing. Her face looked radiant; she was completely relaxed. There was no doubt that she was deep in prayer, no longer conscious of my presence in the room… When she was ready, Sarah opened her eyes. "I feel tired… I want to end here," she said. (66-67)

Though the previous encounter with imagery happened in the context of spiritual direction, it could equally well have happened in life coaching. Sarah's ecstatic state was neither brought on by breath work nor by extensive exploration of her imagery; rather, it was an immediate response to a simple question: *"Do any images come to mind?"* As previously stated, it is very rare for a coaching client to enter the *mysterium* during a coaching session; however, if this were to happen, the best response from the coach would be to remain silent until the client chooses to speak; to interrupt the experience with questions or observations would violate the sacredness of the moment.

As a final comment regarding religious imagery in coaching, it is important to note that because imagery works on the emotions, one can become addicted to the "spiritual high" that can accompany certain symbols:

Images can fill the void when nothing much seems to be happening, spiritually speaking, but sometimes it is necessary to enter that void— to live with it, accept it and learn from it. Relying on images offers comfort, yes, but it can be an obstacle to further growth. Knowing God involves meeting that God who is beyond all images, beyond all experiences, and beyond all techniques to "draw closer." (62)

The coach, then, is best off using **Image Guidance** or imagery in general sparingly, for specific reasons, and with the right clients. While a trip to the *mysterium* may be what the client most desires, it may not necessarily advance his or her coaching agenda! But, then again, it just might!

Moving away from levels of consciousness, the type of religious imagery that surfaces in coaching can also be indicative of the client's spiritual maturity or of what James Fowler names as *"Stages of Faith"* and Richard Barrett names as the *"Seven Stages of Psychological Development."* Both authors examine "soul work" in terms of life stages, describing what might be expected at a particular chronological age.

Fowler's stages, for example, range from the fantasy-filled *Intuitive-Projective Faith* (child 3-7) to the transcendent, completely-altruistic *Universalizing Faith* achieved by the rare few (Gandhi, Mother Teresa, Thomas Merton). A client's imagery will reveal whether he or she is still operating at a child's level of faith, clinging to inherited beliefs without reflection, or at a more adult level of faith which has evolved through the process of individuation and may include the understanding that truth is multi-dimensional.

Fowler's Mrs. W. illustrates this point well (146-147). A woman in her fifties, she views prayer as an investment that she regularly deposits in a spiritual bank account, to be drawn upon as needed; this imagery shows a literal-magical understanding of faith which she has passed on to her adult children. Faith is transactional: she invests and God, a "bank teller" who can be placated by financial deposits, re-pays! How one coaches Mrs. W. will be very different than how one might coach a Mother Teresa who viewed herself as a "pencil in the hand of God!"

Knowing the client's primary image of God can help the spiritual coach ask the powerful questions that can open someone up to a deeper level of faith. A conversation with Mrs. W. could go something like this:

COACH: "If God is like a bank teller, how do you pray?"

MRS. W: "Well, I remind God about all my deposits and know that He is keeping an accurate record that will guarantee me a place in heaven. A little like Santa Claus, I suppose."

COACH: "What would happen if you miss making a deposit?"

MRS. W: "I don't think it would matter if this were just every now and again, but if it became a habit, I could find myself being sent off with the goats."

COACH: *"The goats?"*

MRS. W: "Yes, you know – the people who get sent to hell because they are sinners. I wouldn't want to end up in fire and brimstone, would I?"

COACH: "No, probably not. I wouldn't want to go there, either! But let's explore this further. Imagine you are having a conversation with God and you've just missed making three deposits in a row. What would God say to you?"

MRS. W: "He'd tell me to get over with the goats."

COACH: "And what would a God of Love say to you?"

MRS. W: "He'd say, 'Come and join my sheep.'"

COACH: "What would you have to do to join the sheep."

[PAUSE]

MRS. W: "Nothing. I wouldn't have to do a thing."

COACH: "What has happened to all your deposits?"

MRS. W: "I may be wrong, but I don't think a loving God would need my prayers. I would still pray, of course, but He wouldn't be keeping track or closing the door on me if I became lazy."

Since this is an imaginary coaching session, there is no telling what will happen next; however, Mrs. W. has already had a shift in thinking and seems drawn towards the image of God as Love. This could very well mean that she can now move beyond having a "transactional" relationship with God where God rewards her for her devotions, towards a relationship grounded in God's unconditional Love. Her previous image of God prevented her from growing in faith. Sadly, this is not uncommon. Many "grown-ups," in fact, never advance much beyond the religion they were taught as children. As a result, some eventually walk away from their faith because it is inconsistent with what they know to be true of the world, while others blindly adhere to limiting images and beliefs that may be more superstitious than spiritual.

In contrast, Mother Teresa's level of faith is beautifully expressed in her image of *"a pencil in the hand of God."* As *"pencil,"* she surrendered completely to God who could now write through her. The image evokes a sense of love, trust, and humility; any work that Mother Teresa accomplished was God working through her precisely because of her self-abandonment.

Recently, I gave a workshop for lectors at a Chicago parish and, for some reason, quoted Mother Teresa. I stated that being a "pencil in the hand of God" was a great image but that to me it felt rather cold and thin; I then asked the group to see what they would say— for my part, nothing came as "microphone" and "computer" didn't quite work. Someone suggested a musical instrument which I liked, but it didn't resonate fully. Well, then the answer came: *putty.* I objected and said I would prefer to be clay in the hands of the Potter; that felt more dignified. As we processed this image, someone observed that clay hardens whereas putty is pliable, especially silly putty. I responded that "silly putty" felt like a bit of a put-down. Then came further insight: God was the Child playing with the putty; that's why the putty was silly. That worked!

CHAPTER SIX:
IMAGERY AND THE CORPORATE SETTING

In a corporate setting, working with imagery may seem less appropriate than in life coaching with a private client. An "internal coach" who has already earned the trust of the corporation and its employees may have a certain degree of freedom experimenting with imagery and other tools; however, an "external coach" who has been hired from outside the corporation to help bring about a specific outcome (as for example, improved team spirit, greater productivity and better communication) may feel the pressure of having to "deliver" by a certain date. Armed with assessment tools and strategies for leadership development, the external coach may be less willing to take risks or to engage in any coaching practices that might be perceived as "time wasters." This hesitation may be valid, and first impressions of the corporate culture could very well reflect this. Though the coach may be working with individuals from *within* the corporation, the "client" is whoever pays the bill. The coach, answerable to the "real" client's agenda, therefore has to ensure that the client is satisfied. (For the sake of clarity, in this chapter, I will refer to the person being coached as the "coachee" to distinguish him/her from the "real" client).

This does not mean that there is no scope for using imagery in a corporate setting. Instead of introducing **Image Guidance** as a tool, the coach can simply work with the coachee's symbols and metaphors— and do so effectively! Corporate language, is, in fact, full of imagery. Typically, the types of images that surface are related to sports, construction, transportation, military activity, technology and other male-dominated fields. Of course, there is no way either coach or coachee can control the symbolic imagination, but the images and metaphors that surface in conversation tend to reflect corporate culture: they are *"macho,"* team-based, and outcome-focused; they may also seem cliché and impersonal. Take, for example, the following exchanges which come about when the coach responds to the coachee's utterances:

COACHEE: "I feel **blocked.**"

COACH: "What is **blocking** your way forward?

***

COACHEE: "There are no **bridges** in place."

COACH: "What **bridges** do you need to build?"

***

COACHEE: "The basic **building blocks** are mostly missing."

COACH: "What **building blocks** do you need?"

***

COACHEE: "All I can see are **closed doors.**"

COACH: "What **doors** have opened so far?"

***

COACHEE: "I'm stuck on the **sidelines**."

COACH: "How do you intend to get back in **the game**?"

***

COACHEE: "We **scored a goal** and then **the ball was dropped.**"

COACH: "Who **dropped the ball**?"

***

COACHEE: "We missed **the bullseye**."

COACH: "What's your **target** audience?"

***

COACHEE: "My new assistant manager is a **maverick**."

COACH: "How can you **rope him in**?"

***

In each exchange, the coach is quick to ask a question based on the coachee's metaphors. Each question is startlingly direct and has the potential to jolt the coachee out of his or her limiting mindset. Instead of focusing on the coachee's feelings of being blocked, the coach asks for a definition of the blockage; with the definition in place, it is possible to look at ways of either dismantling this blockage or going around it. When the coachee complains that there are no bridges in place or that basic building blocks are missing, the coach turns this around by asking the coachee what he or she is going to do about this.

Instead of being a helpless victim, the coachee now has a mission to accomplish. In the reference to "closed doors," the coach steers the coachee away from negative thinking into seeing the good developments that have occurred: some doors may be closed, but others may have opened without the coachee even having noticed. The coach in these exchanges doesn't miss a beat; s/he is both direct and challenging without being confrontational. The metaphors, in fact, allow the coach to disrupt previous patterns of thought and misleading claims, thus creating new opportunities for moving forward.

Let's expand on one of these conversations:

COACHEE: "We scored a goal and then the ball was dropped."

COACH: "Who dropped the ball?"

COACHEE: "It's difficult to tell. One minute we were in a winning position and, the next, our competitor got the contract.

COACH: "What goal did you score?"

COACHEE: "Well, our bid made it to the top—it was a contract to replace all the standard thermal pane windows in the State Capitol building with bullet-proof, riot-proof glass. The multi-million-dollar contract was on the governor's desk, awaiting her signature."

COACH: "That's an accomplishment— so what happened?"

COACHEE: "It seems there was a mistake in our estimate based on the number of windows."

COACH: "Sorry – I'm lost here. Please explain what this means."

COACHEE: "Well, an extra zero on the number of windows meant that our bid was twice as high as our competitor's. Instead of contacting us for clarification, they went with the other guy."

COACH: "Who was responsible for reviewing the contract before submitting it?

COACHEE: "I guess that would be my department."

COACH: "You mean, *everyone* in your department?'

COACHEE: "No— I got to do the final review."

COACH: "So who dropped the ball?"

COACHEE: "I guess *I* may have done."

In this exchange, the coach not only pays attention to the metaphor of a ball dropped during an unspecified ballgame, but also to the use of the passive voice. By using the passive — *"The ball was dropped"*— the coachee avoids naming the person ultimately responsible for the loss of the contract. There is definite evasiveness in the coachee's language, as well as a tendency to blame: *"Instead of contacting us for clarification, **they** went with the other guy."* By insisting on clarification around the metaphor, the coach succeeds in helping the coachee finally admit responsibility for the lost contract. Now they can have a *real* conversation.

At this point, the coach has the option to move forward without the metaphor:

COACH: "Moving forward, what might you do differently in the future?"

On the other hand, the coach might decide to stay with the metaphor:

COACH: "Moving forwards, imagine yourself holding that ball, with the whole team depending on you. What would be a game-changer?"

The advantage of staying with the metaphor is that it provides a buffer between the coachee and possible feelings of guilt. Having been caught in evasiveness, the coachee might be embarrassed or have a sense of shame. In all likelihood, this might be the first time that he or she has admitted responsibility for the lost contract. The game imagery removes some of the sting, creating a sense of play while maintaining a serious agenda. At this point, having moved from evasiveness to authenticity, the coachee might even be ready for deeper imagery work. The conversation might continue this way:

COACHEE: "Okay, I'm clutching the ball and all around me I see my team, waiting for me to make it to the end zone. I'm frozen in place. My fingers are sweaty— I'm out of breath and know I can't make the run. The defense is drawing in, and I'm still frozen, terrified I'm going to drop the ball. Then I see Frank— he gets close, on my right, catches my eye— and I make a lateral pass. Crazy, perhaps, but he makes the catch and runs with the ball. We score."

COACH: "What just happened?"

COACHEE: "I let Frank —that's my assistant manager— take on more responsibility, carry the ball. I don't have to carry the game by myself."

COACH: "And what is the advantage of this?"

COACHEE: "If I'm less stressed out, I will make fewer mistakes. Two pairs of eyes are better than one, right?"

COACH: "Absolutely! So what are your next steps?"

Through visualization, the coachee imagines new possibilities. Whereas his or her leadership was previously "top down," now the coachee is somewhat willing to delegate, at least where Frank is concerned. Further coaching could very well open the coachee to a more collaborative model of team leadership. The "dropped ball" serves as a reminder that one person cannot assume all responsibilities without mistakes happening along the way. Moreover, further coaching may also help the coachee move *beyond* delegating to avoid errors, into "power-sharing" as a means of empowering the team. Ideally, the coaching experience will enable him/her to see the desirability of shared leadership instead of the dominator model that is presently in existence. What began as a costly mistake could be a "game changer" for the whole department, and possibly for the company. Had the coach ignored the coachee's use of figurative language, such progress would have been unlikely.

Let's turn now to the maverick imagery:

COACHEE: "My new assistant manager is a **maverick**."

COACH: "How can you **rope him in**?"

Here, the coach needs to ask a clarifying question: what does the term "maverick" mean to the coachee? Though it is probable the coachee is complaining about the new assistant manager, it is also possible that s/he admires mavericks and is actually praising him; the coach cannot simply assume that the coachee is making a derogatory comment. This is where the coach needs to listen deeply to tone of voice and any other markers of attitude; the coach also needs to monitor his/her own attitudes towards mavericks to avoid projecting personal viewpoints onto the coachee's imagery. Here are two different scenarios: in the first, the coach mistakenly assumes the coachee is displeased with the new assistant manager and, in the second, the coach seeks clarification before focusing on the maverick metaphor:

COACHEE: "My new assistant manager is a maverick."

COACH: "How can you rope him in?"

COACHEE: "I've no intention of roping him in—he's an asset to the company."

COACH: "Oh, I assumed he was some kind of uncontrollable Lone Ranger."

COACHEE: "Not at all. He's the best guy on the team."

Caught in an erroneous assumption, the coach now has to re-group. Already, in this very brief exchange, there is a defensiveness in the coachee's responses. As a "one time" error, this should not negatively impact the coach/coachee relationship, but it does reflect a failure in listening on the coach's part. Moreover, should such failures be frequent, then the coachee is going to feel alienated rather than supported: if the coach "doesn't get it," the coachee will share less, trust less, and invest less. It would have been far better in the first scenario had the coach made a standard coaching request: *"Please say more about this,"* or *"What does this mean to you?"*

Let's see where the second scenario will take us:

COACHEE: "My new assistant manager is a maverick."

COACH: "Please explain what you mean by this."

COACHEE: "Well, he's got all the traits of a successful entrepreneur. He thinks outside the box pretty much most of the time and is always open to new ideas— never satisfied with the same old ideas. Reminds me of Steve Jobs— creative, imaginative, a little controversial, willing to take risks even when others try to shut him down. He takes the team where we need to go by breaking the rules but not in a way I'd describe as reckless. He always focusses on the big picture and on the well-being of the company and of our client base. Oh, and he has 'stay with it' power— perseveres until he achieves the outcome he's looking for."

COACH: "It sounds as though you are pretty impressed with this guy."

COACHEE: "Absolutely—this is precisely why I hired him. The problem is upper management. They never take risks which is why we had zero-growth before Frank joined the company. I'm frightened we're going to lose him, if they continue trying to rope him in."

COACH: "What do you think a maverick might need?"

COACHEE: "Not sure— independence, perhaps."

COACH: "That's a good guess. I seem to remember that the original mavericks were horses owned by the Maverick family and that they were identified precisely because they'd never been branded."

COACHEE: "Yeah, I recall something like that."

COACH: "If you're comfortable doing this, I invite you to close your eyes and visualize a maverick running free on the plains. Ask it what it needs to be happy."

COACHEE: *"Ask it?"*

COACH: "Yes. It should say something."

COACHEE: "I just get a few words: autonomy, respect, personal space, support …"

COACH: "That's good! How can you ensure that Frank has these needs met?"

The remainder of the coaching session might focus on how the coachee can protect the new assistant manager from upper management. Instead of "roping in" Frank, the coachee needs to extend the rope his assistant manager already has, thereby allowing for further creativity and increased production. His/her task as manager is to empower rather than stifle this invaluable employee while finding ways for justifying Frank's sometimes unorthodox strategies to "top brass." Since this agenda might take several sessions, at this point the coach and coachee may want to renegotiate the best use of their time together. Of course, if the "client" financing the coaching is upper management, then, for obvious reasons, this may need to be a verbal agreement rather than a written document.

One final comment about using imagery in a corporate setting. As stated earlier, there is no controlling the symbolic imagination and so there are times when the imagery that surfaces may seem curiously out of place. One example of this turns up in Bill Gates' *Rolling Stone* interview (2014) where he is quoted as saying, *"**If I could wave a wand and fix one thing,** it'd be political deadlock, the education system or health care costs. One of those three, I don't know which."* Here, corporate language gives way to fairy tale imagery, with Bill Gates as the "Good Fairy." True, this was an interview and not a coaching session, but as a magic wand surfaced in *Rolling Stone*, so, too, it might surface in corporate coaching. The lesson here is not to be surprised by anything and to be prepared for everything!

CHAPTER SEVEN:
IMAGE GUIDANCE & HEALING

While I have used **Image Guidance** primarily with clients seeking inner healing, much of my use of imagery has either involved working with clients suffering from specific illnesses and disabilities, or else training medical professionals on how to use the process in their own healing practice. Just as I am not a mental health professional, so I must disclaim any formal credentialing as a physical healer. My work with imagery has been intuitive, with the process presenting itself from "nowhere," as a gift from the universe. In *Image Guidance: A Tool for Spiritual Direction,* I explain how one of my own experiences with imagery ultimately saved my son (at that time, thirteen years old) from drowning and then led to my understanding ways of using imagery in therapeutic contexts (3). Rather than leave new readers with a "cliffhanger," I will abbreviate the story. If you have read my earlier version of this, please bear with me!

What happened defies logic and might come across as absurd as many miracle stories do; in fact, I always share this narrative with some reluctance as it does demand that the listener suspend disbelief and accept a world in which the miraculous is possible. One day, while praying, I saw the image of a red and white plastic Jesus (a very garish statue) reaching out its hand to someone who was drowning – a colorless pencil sketch of a boy with his mouth open in a scream, arms flailing in the air. The image would not go away, so I abandoned trying to pray and did something practical instead – like vacuuming or grading student papers. The next day, thinking nothing of the image, I took my children to the beach at Michigan City, IN, along with our friend, Ruth, who was in her eighties. We parked the car, unloaded swim gear and picnic supplies and then considered options: the beach was divided into two sections – one with lifeguards where only paddling was permitted and one without lifeguards where everyone was swimming with carefree abandon. At the second site, however, there was an ominous sign: "WARNING! DEATH MAY OCCUR!" Vaguely disturbed by the sign, I decided we would swim where there were no restrictions, but that we would stay within our depth.

That proved to be the wrong decision. Within minutes of entering the lake, my son was caught in a riptide. The more he tried to swim back towards shore, the further the waves carried him out. I screamed at Ruth to grab my daughter, Alexia, and return to shore; then, instead of swimming after Peter, I waded in up to my waist, planted my feet in the sand, stretched out my hand and told him to come to me. Panicking, he screamed out that he couldn't swim against the current, that he was drowning; trying to stay calm, I reassured him that he was going to be fine and then, unexpectedly, the wind must have shifted because a sudden wave propelled him in my direction. Our fingers met and, holding each other tightly, we somehow dragged ourselves to shore, fighting the relentless current all the way. When we eventually collapsed on the sand, I knew, in a flash, that it was the image of the plastic Jesus that had guided me to stretch out my hand to Peter instead of attempting to swim after him; in a flash, I also knew that imagery could be used in spiritual guidance and that this was work to which I was being called.

Shortly after this experience, I developed my seven-step process and began honing my practical skills with the aid of faculty, staff and student volunteers at DePaul University. Over the years, the clients with whom I have worked have helped advance applications for **Image Guidance** through their own unique circumstances, insights, and needs. I am most at home in the spiritual arena but have also ventured into physical healing. Aware of my limited medical knowledge, however, I will only take on clients for physical healing if they are already under a doctor's care:

> Ideally, I see this application of **Image Guidance** being used by health professionals with their patients and not as a dimension of Spiritual Direction. However, if the illness itself involves spiritual issues (as many illnesses tend to do), then there might be an occasion for a spiritual guide to help the client understand some dimensions of the illness which the medical profession may 'miss.' I strongly urge that spiritual guides simply 'guide': to over-step one's expertise by giving advice about medical concerns could have life-threatening results. (94)

My first explorations of **Image Guidance** and physical healing began with a faculty member at DePaul University, Dr. Judith-Rae Ross. When Judith volunteered to try imagery as a healing tool, she was already under the care of a medical team for "out of control" diabetes. Nothing seemed to work, and she had daily insulin reactions; in fact, at the start of each semester, she always had to inform her students about how to handle an insulin emergency and when to call the paramedics. With the permission of her medical team, Judith and I began working together. What followed was an amazing journey in which Judith moved from seeing her diabetes as "enemy" to learning to live in harmony with it. Here is Judith's account of her experience, excerpted from *Image Guidance: A Tool for Spiritual Direction:*

Dear Liz:

Funny, but when you first asked me what I thought of when I thought of my diabetes, I had always thought of the word, "diabetes." It was in yellow cartoon script with pinkish, orange and blue outlines around the yellow letters. But once I thought of it as a thing, the large purple, oblong blob I described popped into my mind. It was as if the diabetes unmasked itself. The diabetes isn't a simple purple blob. It is purple in places, but in other places, it is brownish purple, the color of my potassium pills. Still, in other places, it is crusted over with a lead glass diamond finish, quite elegant.

In the process of imaging, I became quite relaxed. It was as if some of the cares I carry around had been lifted, and I became more and more focused upon the diabetes. I seemed to be communicating with it rather than fighting, and I felt all my stress leaving me, flowing out of me. I felt myself slowing down, and I felt the insulin reaction I was fighting ease....

While I was imaging, things just kept popping into my mind. The answers and insights were suddenly there. Yet while they flashed into my mind, I was feeling very relaxed, focused and euphoric. I felt at peace. It was almost a religious experience.

Imaging has helped me to become more attuned to what the diabetes needs. I want to do it again and learn more. This may ramble a bit, but the process has helped me calm myself and express what the illness has meant to me. Just giving my diabetes a shape and color has pulled it in focus. Just knowing that it wants to teach me something, and that it's not my total enemy is a big step for me.

Thank you!

Judith

From her dialogues with the purple blob (whose name, by the way, was *Elmo Elijah*) Judith learned to slow down and relax. At times, she asked her image for guidance on such matters as diet, exercise and medication, testing its responses with her supportive medical team. Over time, her blood sugars stabilized, and medical emergencies became a rare occurrence. Imagery, then, became the life-line that brought Judith's diabetes under control.

In the years that followed, I worked with numerous clients facing physical limitations; in most cases, once the client could remember the onset of his or her condition, symptoms either disappeared totally or else became more manageable. The range of physical ailments was truly extraordinary: individuals with carpal tunnel syndrome who learned to delegate and thereby avoided surgery; women with food addictions who traced their eating disorders back to either a situation of rape or molestation, often incestuous; clients with "temporary paralysis" who regained the use of their limbs once they made the connection between feeling marginalized and their loss of motion; clients with gastric disorders who recognized that they couldn't "stomach life" because they were not leading lives that would bring them happiness and fulfillment; two women whose acute migraines had begun decades before, following abortions; people dealing with chronic pain that turned out to be stress-related....

In each case, I insisted that my clients should consult their medical caregivers before making any decisions regarding a change in their treatment, but the results were consistent: increased peace of mind, improved quality of life, reduced medication, and, in several situations, the avoidance of surgery. In some cases, clients made major lifestyle adjustments such as changing careers or leaving destructive relationships; in others, once they understood the roots of their physical ailments, clients began to work with dieticians, physiotherapists, and other specialists. My approach, however, did rely on going into the past and exploring the issues that surfaced; this, of course, is a therapeutic model rather than one appropriate for life coaching. Moreover, it often involved using breath work to achieve altered states of consciousness rather than mere relaxation, and sessions could last anywhere from thirty minutes to two hours –again, signaling "inappropriateness" for life coaching.

All this being said, I do believe that **Image Guidance** can be used as a "healing tool" within life coaching; the guidelines are simply that interventions should be brief, safe and forward-focusing. In addition, the coach needs to stay within his or her area of competency, leaving diagnosis and remedies to medical professionals, and never making suggestions that undermine existing protocols. *Applications?* A few that immediately come to mind include assisting the client:

- deal with chronic pain, transcend fear, or prepare for unpleasant or painful medical procedures such as surgery, skin grafts and chemotherapy;
- prepare for childbirth;
- accept chronic conditions and their accompanying limitations;
- adjust to loss (e.g. loss of speech or vision, loss of a limb, loss of reproductive ability, loss of cognitive skills, loss of looks, etc.);
- live in harmony with irreversible conditions such as paralysis;

- see the spiritual dimensions of his or her medical condition and become an active participant in the recovery process;
- move beyond trauma and into a future that is as productive and fulfilling as possible.

To illustrate the use of imagery for physical healing in life-coaching contexts, I have adapted two case studies from *Image Guidance and Healing,* shortening them to what I would consider an appropriate length for a life coaching session. The first involves Carmen, an obstetrics nurse in her early forties who was close to giving birth to her first child; she was terrified not only of the pain but also of humiliating herself by fighting her caregivers, some of whom would be her peers from the hospital where she worked. She had scheduled a coaching appointment to help develop coping skills for the actual labor/delivery.

I began the session by leading Carmen through a simple breathing exercise, inviting her to breathe out tension, fear and anxiety and to breathe in confidence, strength and peace of mind. Since she knew she was having a boy, we had agreed that she would dialogue with her unborn child.

COACH: "Carmen, focus on the image of your little boy and then describe what you can see."

CARMEN: "I can see… his hair… and it's very soft and fine… I can see his eyes starting to open… I can see his hands stretching upward and his feet in the air… and I can see myself holding him, wrapping him against me in my robe. He feels warm and peaceful, and it feels right."

COACH: "What other feelings have surfaced for you?"

CARMEN: "I feel happy and anxious and excited … and all kinds of feelings of being afraid and hopeful. I feel a stronger connection to life. I am a part of what I see around me."

COACH: "Carmen, can you say more about this sense of connection you now experience?"

CARMEN: "I guess when I look at myself going through the process of labor, I see myself accepting help from other people, though I always have a hard time being weak. I see myself being vulnerable without humiliation, and this allows me to have more to give the child that's coming. If I recognize my neediness, I can recognize his neediness, too."

COACH: "Carmen, ask your unborn child how he feels about the birth process."

CARMEN: "He says he wants to stay in the womb because it's warm and comfortable. There's excitement and fear of the unknown. He is filled with fear, anxiety and hope…"

COACH: "He sounds just like you do! If you're comfortable doing this, ask your child how you can make his journey into this world easier."

CARMEN: "He says… (laughter) … The vision I get in my mind is the scene in *Star Wars* where Obi-Wan Kenobi dies, and Luke Skywalker is in a spaceship, speeding down a canal, fighting –it reminds me of the birth canal. Obi-Wan says, 'Let's go, Luke. Let the Force be with you.' I guess that's what the baby's saying to me. 'Let go. The Force is with you.' He tells me to relax, not to fight my body but to let it do what it knows how to do and he says to trust in the process and let go. I need to stay in the moment…"

COACH: "How will you do this?"

CARMEN: "Hmm… I don't know. Somehow in life (not just in labor), I tend to brace myself for what will happen. I have this false idea that if I brace myself, it will be less painful. But it's not."

COACH: "Ask the child for advice. Perhaps he can offer some insight here."

CARMEN: "He says I should talk to the people around me who are trained to help me. I should listen to their guidance with an open mind before I panic and say I can't stand it. And if I become angry, I should use my anger to empower me rather than to shove people away. I need to look forward to the first meeting of my child, myself and my husband."

COACH: "How does this advice make you feel?"

CARMEN: "Stronger. It makes me feel stronger. It makes me feel a willingness and a feeling of surrender. It makes me feel as if I don't need to struggle with myself and that peace will come if I stop fighting my body."

COACH: "You need to remember all that your child has taught you. You need to remember your strength and your will. Thank your son for everything you have learned and then, when you are ready, open your eyes."

As the session concluded, I noticed that Carmen seemed entirely peaceful. The tension had gone, replaced instead by a sense of joyful anticipation. While she was under no illusion that **Image Guidance** would be a substitute for anesthesia, she did know that it would help her stay centered during the days before her child's arrival and possibly through labor itself.

Though I have shortened Carmen's case study, the only real difference between the original session and what I would do in a life coaching session is the length of the imagery intervention. Breath-work has its place in both therapy and life coaching; moreover, dialoguing with an unborn child is also appropriate in both contexts. Both sessions were more about the future than the past, and both invited the client to find the empowerment to move forwards, beyond fear. Most importantly, each session provided an imaginative tool that Carmen could use on her own, during labor and delivery.

The second case study involves Dan, a Catholic seminarian who was seeing me for spiritual direction; he developed a mysterious ailment which afflicted his right arm, leaving him in acute pain and unable to perform ordinary activities such as writing, driving or playing the piano. After X-rays, bone scans, blood tests, C-T scans and an MRI, neither he nor his doctors were any the wiser as to what was going on. I explained **Image Guidance** to him, and he was willing to give it a try.

COACH: "Dan, are there any images that describe how you are feeling?"

DAN: "Well, I feel as though I've been zapped by a lightning bolt. Or perhaps a huge jaw has chomped down on my wrist— as in *Jaws,* the movie."

COACH: "You are describing *externalized* pain. What image do you have of your *internal* pain?"

DAN: "I feel boxed in. Helpless. Squashed in. The lid is heavy, and there's no way of raising it."

COACH: "What do you look like, squished in that box?"

DAN: "A skeleton in a womb. Anguished. All in black. My knees are crunched; my back is bent. I'm tense, insecure breathing fast, panting…"

COACH: "Dan, ask the box how you got inside it."

DAN: "It says, 'You walked in. You volunteered. You let yourself be hurt. Your fear is what keeps you from having enough power to raise the lid."

COACH: "Ask the box how you can escape."

DAN: "It says, 'You can dissolve my walls, but I won't tell you how. You can unlock all the locks, but you have to figure out which keys to use.'"

COACH: "Dan, ask the lid how you can raise it."

DAN: "It says, 'You have to use your mind, not your muscles. You will have to know when it's the right time.'"

COACH: "What else do you hear?"

DAN: "I have all the knowledge I need. From now on, it's my responsibility— the box isn't going to help!"

COACH: "Ask the box where you can find the strength to deal with this situation."

DAN: "I have to look to the deepest place inside. I have to use both my deepest emotions and my mind. Using just my emotions or my mind is not enough. Both are needed."

COACH: "What is holding you back?"

DAN: "The box says, 'You have let your past write your present and your future. You let old fears guide your present. Part of you has grown up, and yet you still hold on to old fears that aren't you anymore."

COACH: "If you are comfortable doing this, Dan, ask the box to name your fears."

DAN: "Embarrassment, failure in the eyes of others, saying the wrong thing, saying nothing, giving up before seeing something through…"

COACH: "Ask the box how you can overcome these fears."

DAN: "By focusing on my strengths, by working on what's already good, by giving myself time for healing …"

COACH: "Ask the box what happened to your hand."

DAN: "It says that the pain in my hand is showing me that I'm not caring for my whole self. I have to put my needs first and others' needs second. It says I've been tense so long and clenched so long that my hand can't relax. I push too hard and put deadlines over what I know to be healthy for myself."

COACH: "So your hand is overworked?"

DAN: "It's been overworked and overworked and overworked for years. It's forcing me to listen."

COACH: "Dan, what are you going to do about this situation?"

DAN: "I have to listen to all my pains. I have to stop working when the pain starts. I need to focus on relaxing my whole body, not just parts. I must not simply wait for crises to take time out."

COACH: "Dan, your hand will be made whole when you learn to love yourself and when you take better care of yourself. Your hand will be healed when you accept yourself in all your strengths and limitations. The pain you have experienced is a symptom of deeper pain which is demanding attention. Let's discuss next steps…."

As in the previous case study, I have merely shortened this transcript rather than adjust it specifically for life coaching. Intuition and my previous work with this client guided me to focus more on inner pain than external pain; somehow, I knew from the outset that Dan's issues were psychological/emotional/spiritual rather than physical, but I was more interested in a solution than in going to the root of Dan's limiting issues. In other words, I wanted to use imagery as a tool for moving forwards rather than for dwelling on the past. Instead of focusing on fear, embarrassment and the other limitations that surfaced, I directed Dan to ask the box/lid for solutions. In retrospect, my approach comes across as more directive than is customary in life coaching, but my tone of voice is always invitational. I would also add that when using imagery, the coach/guide is rather like a stage director and so a "directive" presence is often necessary.

Regarding "next steps," we looked at physiotherapy, prayer and time to relax. At the seminary, Dan paid more attention to his own inner life and academic performance and less on how he compared to his classmates. Once he understood that he himself held the keys to his well-being, he was on the road to healing.

CHAPTER EIGHT:
GETTING STARTED

For coaches who are used to more traditional ways of engaging clients, the idea of using **Image Guidance** as a technique may be intimidating. After all, when we allow imagery to guide our coaching conversations, we are in the territory of the unpredictable and, to be quite honest, the ridiculous. Many years ago, after I had written *Image Guidance: A Tool for Spiritual Direction*, I began working on a sequel with healthcare applications. At the time, I was serving as a University Minister/ Religious Studies faculty member at *DePaul University*; I therefore took advantage of my campus connections to see if there were students with disabilities who would be willing to help me advance my work. The one and only student who volunteered later admitted she had done so for "a lark"; confined to a wheelchair following a car accident, she had become a detached critic of the outer world and saw an opportunity to have fun at my expense. Ironically, over the course of a year we covered some amazing territory together, becoming good friends in the process; in fact, I ended up dedicating the book to her.

Having conversations with images that surface from the unconscious takes a leap of faith, both for the coach and for the client. In the first place, it is essential that the coach is a "true believer." Without a healthy respect for imagery and creative imaginative guiding, a coach should not experiment with imagery. This was the premise behind the ICF-approved course I designed for the *Institute for Life Coach Training*. Simply entitled, *Image Guidance for Life Coaches*, the course offers students opportunities to 1). learn about imagery and its coaching applications; and 2). to experience **Image Guidance** and to put it into practice under supervision.

This chapter will present authentic transcripts (used with permission) that demonstrate the learning process. For the sake of anonymity and readability, I will use the terms **"STUDENT COACH," "CLIENT"** and **"INSTRUCTOR."** I should point out, however, that the "student coaches" are fully-credentialed coaches with their own unique practices. The instructions for the assignment were as follows:

Preparing the Verbatim (or Transcript of Coaching Session)

*First of all, this is not a graded assignment and does not have to be a literary work or even grammatically correct! What is needed is a "reasonably accurate" record of a section of your Coaching Session that focuses on using imagery. It would be very helpful to your classmates if you could send your transcript to the class the day **before** our next meeting, so we can all have a chance to read it. We will use the transcripts and your peer feedback as the basis for each class. You could take notes during your phone coaching session provided this doesn't distract you from deep listening. When coaching in person, it may be better to reconstruct the session **after** it comes to a close, rather than run the risk of making the client self-conscious or of interrupting the "flow." Also, the sound of rustling papers can be very distracting!*

Here is the suggested format, but please don't let this limit you in terms of your response:

DATE:

TIME:

TYPE OF SESSION: phone or in person

TYPE OF CLIENT: actual client, volunteer or classmate

CLIENT'S AGENDA: one or two sentences

WHY YOU FELT IMAGERY WOULD HELP CLIENT: one or two sentences

ACTUAL EXCHANGE BETWEEN COACH AND CLIENT:

Coach:

Client:

Coach:

Client:

Etc.

BRIEF SUMMARY REGARDING THE EFFECTIVENESS OF THE SESSION. STRENGTHS? WHAT WOULD YOU DO DIFFERENTLY? CLIENT FEEDBACK, IF ANY?

***

TRANSCRIPT ONE (with instructor comments)

DATE: 8/4/14

TIME: 11:30 a.m.

TYPE OF SESSION: phone

TYPE OF CLIENT: classmate

CLIENT'S AGENDA: Client has an issue with an extended family member.

WHY YOU FELT IMAGERY WOULD HELP CLIENT: To

help her to gain more insights to deal with her issue.

ACTUAL EXCHANGE BETWEEN COACH AND CLIENT:

STUDENT COACH: "What are the issues that you want to focus on today?"

CLIENT: "I would like to focus on my relationship with an extended family member."

STUDENT COACH: "What are the issues that you have with the family member?"

CLIENT: "I would like to gain more insight as to whether I could do anything more to have a closer relationship with this family member. She and I have different values."

STUDENT COACH: "May I ask you who is your extended family member?"

CLIENT: "She is my *[client specified her family member]*. She is not a believer, and we are now distanced from each other. She had been baptized in church when she was young. She was recognized for her achievements, but she did something to hurt me."

STUDENT COACH: "If you look at the Carolyn Myss' chart on Chakra issues, where do you see yourself in the chart?"

INSTRUCTOR: Here you already know that your client is familiar with the Chakra chart because we discussed it in class. If you were working with a "regular" client, however, you would make a note of the client's life issues/ physical symptoms and simply be aware of the Chakra Wellness Chart yourself, rather than discussing it with the client. Most of the time,

charts and theories are tools for our use rather than for the client's use.

CLIENT: "I think it's the Fourth Chakra. I have upper back shoulder pain; I also know that I have forgiveness and compassion issues. I feel compassion towards my family member, but I struggle because her actions had hurt me. I feel bitterness toward her as well."

INSTRUCTOR: Here, if the client is open to this, I would see if she can be more specific about what actually happened. This would allow you to go deeper; on the other hand, staying at the surface is a safeguard against ending up with a therapy session instead of coaching. The client's agenda is to see whether she can improve her relationship with her estranged family member, so avoiding probing questions may be appropriate here.

STUDENT COACH: "Close your eyes. What image comes to your mind?"

INSTRUCTOR: If you were working with a client who was unfamiliar with Image Guidance, you would need to briefly explain what you would like to do regarding imagery and ask her permission to use this tool. You ask the client to close her eyes before coming up with an image, but this works because the client has already been descriptive about her feelings. I usually explore the image *before* asking the client to close his/her eyes, but here you are doing just fine.

CLIENT: "A rope in a tug-of-war."

STUDENT COACH: "What is the color of the rope?"

CLIENT: "Brown."

STUDENT COACH: "How do you feel when you touch the rope?"

CLIENT: "It is rough, and it has some pressure."

STUDENT COACH: "Ask the rope what you can you do so it will not feel so rough or make you feel pressure."

CLIENT: "The rope says to let it go."

STUDENT COACH: "Can you ask the rope if it really wants you to let go?"

CLIENT: "Yes."

INSTRUCTOR: Here you ask a YES/NO question, and it is not clear whether the client is saying that she can ask the rope if she should let go, or if the rope is instructing her to let go. You then move on to a different question without addressing what the "yes" means.

STUDENT COACH: "Ask the rope, what will happen to you if you let go?"

CLIENT: "It says, 'you'll be free.'"

INSTRUCTOR: Here the client could ask the rope to explain what it means by "free." Then she could ask whether it would be possible to have a relationship with this family member and whether, in fact, this would be advisable. This was the stated agenda at the beginning of the coaching session and needs to be addressed.

BRIEF SUMMARY REGARDING THE EFFECTIVENESS OF THE SESSION. STRENGTHS? WHAT WOULD YOU DO DIFFERENTLY? CLIENT FEEDBACK, IF ANY?

STUDENT COACH: The client feels that the questions help her understand her issues. She felt that the **Image Guidance** session seemed too fast. She felt that her issue was also a spiritual battle involving compassion *versus* bitterness. When I asked the client what the rope meant to her, she said that the rope in a tug-of-war was her feeling of both bitterness/anger and compassion.

INSTRUCTOR: This is a good start, but needs further conversation, with or without the use of imagery. The imagery has revealed some insights, but now the client needs to process what she has learned. The bottom line is, does she still wish to repair her relationship with her family member? What must she let go? What price will she pay? Is she willing to pay the price?

STUDENT COACH: I asked the client whether she could hold on to the bitterness and angry feeling for a while, and then let it go. The client said that she envisioned herself at both ends of the rope. I said to her that was her choice if she wanted to let the rope go.

INSTRUCTOR: Good! So now you need to help the client set some goals for herself around this issue. What are the next steps?

***

TRANSCRIPT TWO (with instructor comments)

DATE: 8/4/2014

TIME: 8:30 a.m.

TYPE OF SESSION: Phone

TYPE OF CLIENT: Classmate

CLIENT'S AGENDA: Client wanted more insight as to what more he could do to relieve both his stress and his son's stress.

WHY YOU FELT IMAGERY WOULD HELP CLIENT: He was willing and open to gaining more insight.

EXCHANGE BETWEEN COACH AND CLIENT:

STUDENT COACH: "What would you like to focus on today?"

CLIENT: "This morning I'd like to focus on my son. He does not want to go to summer school but just wants to relax."

STUDENT COACH: "Was going to summer school your wish, or did he want to go, too?"

CLIENT: "Both. My son wanted to go to summer school and has already been attending for one month; now he doesn't want to go."

STUDENT COACH: "Has there been any situation that has come up recently to influence his not wanting to go to summer school?"

CLIENT: "Yes, our move, all the unpacking. The drive is longer— it adds to the stress."

STUDENT COACH: "Yes, that would be stressful. What one thing would you like to take away from this session?"

CLIENT: "I want to know what to do…more free time, going to the beach… I want more insight regarding what else I could do to relieve both our stress."

STUDENT COACH: "Okay, I invite you to close your eyes. As you bring to mind your son and all the stress you are both facing, what image comes to your mind?"

INSTRUCTOR: If you have worked with this client before, you may know the "back story" about the move as well as details about his son's age, personality, etc. I would definitely need more detailed background information before working with imagery.

CLIENT: "The beach, playing ball."

STUDENT COACH: "Is it just you and your son, or is your whole family there?"

INSTRUCTOR: The client never said that he was at the beach. He mentions a beach and someone playing ball but never names that person or people. Remember to check rather than assume!

CLIENT: "The whole family is there, but right now I'm just seeing me and my son."

STUDENT COACH: "What kind of ball are you playing with?"

CLIENT: "It has different colors, red, blue, etc. It's light, and we're throwing it in the air."

STUDENT COACH: "How is your son looking now?"

CLIENT: "We are both happy."

INSTRUCTOR: Here you need to stay with the client's experience and "unpack it" in as much detail as you can. You might have asked, "How can you tell that you are both happy?" Or, "What does it feel like to be happy?"

STUDENT COACH: "Ask the ball how you can keep this light moment, even after you leave the beach?"

CLIENT: "Play more, hold onto me more."

INSTRUCTOR: What does the client mean by "hold onto me more"?

STUDENT COACH: "Ask the ball how you can keep a balance, playing more and still doing things that need to be done?"

CLIENT: "Don't worry, be happy."

INSTRUCTOR: Here again you need to explore what the client's reply means. Your client gives very brief answers, so it is important to stay with his experience.

STUDENT COACH: "If you feel comfortable, imagine you are still playing ball with your son. How do you feel?"

CLIENT: "Relaxed, light, stress-free."

STUDENT COACH: "I invite you to feel this relaxation. You can play with your son anytime and feel that light and stress-free moment. [Pause] When you're ready, open your eyes."

CLIENT: "Okay."

BRIEF SUMMARY REGARDING THE EFFECTIVENESS OF THE SESSION. STRENGTHS? WHAT WOULD YOU DO DIFFERENTLY? CLIENT FEEDBACK, IF ANY?

STUDENT COACH: We processed and discussed the session. The client said that he knew what to do from the start but now feels that instead of just thinking about it, he's going to take action. The client took away next steps of buying a ball and going to the beach with his son. The session was short, but the client felt it was helpful. I should have asked him when he was going to take his next steps.

INSTRUCTOR: Yes, that's an important insight – some accountability is needed! This is the type of brief intervention that I see working well in coaching. The client has a goal which you address; the imagery is simple but gets right to the heart of the matter. The client already knows that he and his son need to play more, but the session has reinforced this. You use Image Guidance in a straightforward way that seems very natural and almost effortless. My only real critique is that you need to stay with the client's experience and explore more details when his answers are so brief.

TRANSCRIPT THREE (with instructor comments)

DATE: 8/12/2014

TIME: 9:00 a.m.

TYPE OF SESSION: Phone

TYPE OF CLIENT: Classmate

CLIENT'S AGENDA: Client wanted insight on what more he could do in the area of self-care.

WHY YOU FELT IMAGERY WOULD HELP CLIENT: He was willing and open to gaining more insight.

<u>**ACTUAL EXCHANGE BETWEEN COACH AND CLIENT:**</u>

STUDENT COACH: "What would you like to focus on today?"

CLIENT: "Summer is almost over; September is coming. I'll be very busy with my children in school, more work at the church, and doing more self-study."

STUDENT COACH: "How does that make you feel?"

CLIENT: "Stressed, not relaxing."

STUDENT COACH: "Sounds like those activities could take a toll on you. What one thing would you like to take away from this session?"

CLIENT: "More insight on how to do self-care, how to be totally relaxed."

STUDENT COACH: "What image comes up for you as you focus on doing more self-care?"

CLIENT: "Lying down on the beach, the sun is shining on me …doing nothing and just relaxing."

STUDENT COACH: "Okay…I invite you to close your eyes. Look at yourself lying down on the beach. Please describe more so I can see it, too."

INSTRUCTOR: Good! Getting details from the client allows "the guide to enter the imagery but also allows the client to go

more deeply into the experience.

CLIENT: "I'm in a beach area, the waves are moving up and down and down. It's hot; the sun is shining. I'm lying down. It feels good to be relaxed."

STUDENT COACH: "Is there anyone else or is it just you?"

CLIENT: "Just me."

STUDENT COACH: "Do you feel or hear anything?"

CLIENT: "Not much. Just the waves."

STUDENT COACH: "Could you ask the waves how you can keep this relaxed feeling even after leaving the beach?"

CLIENT: "Take time relaxing on the beach."

STUDENT COACH: "Ask the waves if there is anything else you can do to stay relaxed."

CLIENT: "Think of nothing."

STUDENT COACH: "Does that make sense to you?"

CLIENT: "Yes."

STUDENT COACH: ": "Sounds like those activities could take a toll! I invite you to feel this relaxation and continue to think of nothing.... When you're ready, open your eyes."

CLIENT: "Okay."

BRIEF SUMMARY REGARDING THE EFFECTIVENESS OF THE SESSION. STRENGTHS? WHAT WOULD YOU DO DIFFERENTLY? CLIENT FEEDBACK, IF ANY?

We processed and discussed the session. The client felt it was important for him to not think of anything, i.e., not have any electronics nearby like a cell phone, computer, etc., to help him relax and help with his self-care. His next step was to schedule a trip to the beach, and he plans to put this on his calendar either today or tomorrow.

The client felt the session was helpful. He felt it would have been easier for him to close his eyes first and then be asked for an image. During the **Image Guidance**, I could have had the client ask the waves how to keep the relaxed feeling even when the weather turns cold, when it's not as feasible to go to the beach. Also, before having the client open his eyes again, I should have recapped some more; for example, I could have said, "I invite you to feel this relaxation, to feel the warm sun on you, to hear the gentle lapping of the waves…."

INSTRUCTOR: Good! If you find it more helpful to have the client close his eyes and then come up with an image, go for it! There is no "right" way of doing this, though, personally, I prefer to have the image before asking clients to close eyes. Your client moved into the imagery quickly, and your questions were just enough to lead him there. With another client, you may need to ask for more details and description. Your analysis is right on target – some good strategies here for another time. When the waves say, "Think of nothing," you might also have asked, "What is usually on your mind?" followed by, "How can you get rid of these worries and concerns?" or "How do these worries and concerns make you feel?" All in all, this was an effective imagery session, very suitable as part of a coaching session.

***

TRANSCRIPT FOUR (with instructor comments)

DATE: 8/5/2014

TIME: 10:00 a.m. EST

TYPE OF SESSION: phone

TYPE OF CLIENT: actual client

CLIENT'S AGENDA: to examine her coaching objectives

WHY YOU FELT IMAGERY WOULD HELP CLIENT:

Because of her background as a psychotherapist, she needed clarity around her coaching style.

ACTUAL EXCHANGE BETWEEN COACH AND CLIENT:

STUDENT COACH: "What would you like your focus for today's session to be?"

CLIENT: "I need to have a clearer focus about my coaching objectives."

STUDENT COACH: "Could you explain more?"

CLIENT: "I was treating a client that had some goals that she was working on, but there seemed to be blockages to her obtaining her goals. My intuition told me to dig deeper. I felt concerned for her safety. I then put on my counseling hat and being a coach, that is not what we are told to do."

INSTRUCTOR: Here more details are needed – what was the specific situation? Why was the coach concerned for her

115

client's safety? Before going into the imagery, you need a clearer understanding of the issue and what the client hopes for regarding an outcome.

STUDENT COACH: "Okay, let us focus on you. Could you close your eyes and take several deep breaths. Then let me know if any images come to mind. Can you tell me what you see?"

CLIENT: "An eagle."

STUDENT COACH: "What is the eagle doing?"

INSTRUCTOR: What does the eagle look like? As many details as possible are needed here!

CLIENT: "It's perched in a tree."

INSTRUCTOR: What is the eagle doing in the tree? You need more descriptive details.

STUDENT COACH: "What is around the eagle? What does the landscape look like?"

CLIENT: "There are trees; the land is mostly flat. The eagle is looking around, it sees... (this portion was difficult to understand because of phone issues)"

INSTRUCTOR: Because you missed some of the client's comments, here it wouldn't hurt to ask, "So could you tell me again what the eagle sees?"

STUDENT COACH: "So is the eagle flying or in a tree?"

CLIENT: "Flying."

STUDENT COACH: "If you were to ask the eagle, where does it want to go, what would it tell you?"

CLIENT: "It is looking around."

STUDENT COACH: "What does it see as it is looking around?"

CLIENT: "Trees, an animal, a butterfly, water."

INSTRUCTOR: These are all symbols of life; water and butterflies are often associated with transformation. It would be worth asking the eagle how it feels when it sees the tree, animal, butterfly, and water.

STUDENT COACH: "Can you ask the eagle what it wants to do?"

CLIENT: "It wants to fly and protect."

STUDENT COACH: "What is it protecting?"

INSTRUCTOR: Here the direct question as opposed to, "Ask the eagle…" moves the client into analytic mode and out of the experience of the imagery. As a result, you move into processing the experience, but this is fine – just be aware of the difference between the direct question (great to bring a session to an end) and a question directed at the image which extends the imagery experience.

CLIENT: "I think the eagle represents myself protecting the innocent; it is focusing on where the butterfly goes."

STUDENT COACH: "What does the butterfly represent?"

CLIENT: "My client. I felt I that I needed to follow my intuition and investigate some of her deeper issues before we could go further with our session. The eagle is me while the butterfly is a beautiful strong being in the world of nature who seems like she's trying to be strong but needs to show someone her fragile side."

BRIEF SUMMARY REGARDING THE EFFECTIVENESS OF THE SESSION. STRENGTHS? WHAT WOULD YOU DO DIFFERENTLY? CLIENT FEEDBACK, IF ANY?

STUDENT COACH: There was some other conversation following this exchange, and then we reviewed the session. We both agreed that this was a productive session. The client concluded that in some circumstances, there may be a need for her to put on a therapist's hat. She is hoping this will not be often, but she has the training to do so and does not feel as guilty as she did before the session.

INSTRUCTOR: This is a positive outcome. We all have tools, and though we should avoid moving into therapeutic mode 99.9% of the time, there may be rare occasions when a brief intervention is necessary. However, we have to be conscious of what we are doing and why, avoiding the trap of making such interventions too frequent. The bottom line is that when a situation arises in which the client needs immediate help, we are usually the only resource on hand!

***

TRANSCRIPT FIVE (with instructor comments)

DATE: 7/16/14

TIME: 10:00 a.m. MT

TYPE OF SESSION: Phone.

TYPE OF CLIENT: Volunteer from a yoga class.

CLIENT'S AGENDA: The client wanted help deciding on steps to take next in her family/relationship.

WHY YOU FELT IMAGERY WOULD HELP CLIENT:

She was very willing, she is open-minded and attends my image guided/spiritually based yoga classes.

<u>ACTUAL EXCHANGE BETWEEN COACH AND CLIENT:</u>

STUDENT COACH: "Hi Client! I'm going to explain what we're going to do in the next 20 minutes or so. I'd love to hear if that sounds okay with you and I'll answer any other questions you may have. After you give me a brief rundown about the decision that you're trying to make, then I am going to lead you into a sort of relaxation like we do in any yoga class. Then we're going to start working with that question and any mental images or pictures that may arise. I'll just ask you questions and see what insights come up during the session."

INSTRUCTOR: Here your explanation could have been a little clearer. You could have explained that the client would keep her eyes closed throughout the experience and that you would facilitate a conversation with her imagery. I like the parallel you draw between Image Guidance and your use of imagery/relaxation in yoga classes.

CLIENT: "That sounds good."

STUDENT COACH: "Great. So tell me a little bit about what's going on for you."

CLIENT: "Well, I've been married for 15 years and been with my husband for 20 years. I'm not quite sure what I want. Should I stay? Is this the best path? We have two kids."

STUDENT COACH: "Can you narrow the question down a little bit more? What's the one question you'd like information about?"

CLIENT: "What's the best path for all of us?"

STUDENT COACH: "Alright, take a moment to close your eyes. Take a deep breath in through your nose, out through your mouth. Notice the sensation of your body sinking into the chair or wherever you are and notice the sensation of your breath. Each breath out allows you to enter this present moment a little bit more. And then come back to that question: what's the best path for all of us? How does that feel in your body? What comes up for you?"

INSTRUCTOR: Excellent lead in to the imagery. Good use of breath work to allow for a shift in consciousness. Good grounding in physical sensations. I would separate the two ending questions. Allow the client to describe what she is experiencing physically, and when she has answered, then ask what comes up for her.

CLIENT: "Change, forgive, except, sacrifice, selfish, self…"

STUDENT COACH: "As you breathe, eyes still closed, thinking about these words, are there any images that come into your mind?"

CLIENT: "All of the places we've lived in, all of the different houses."

STUDENT COACH: "Are there any places that are standing out more than the others?"

CLIENT: "There two places. One before the kids - Alaska by myself, and also a ranch that we lived on with our first child."

STUDENT COACH: "Which one is the most present for you?"

INSTRUCTOR: I like the way you narrow down all the places where the client has lived. This allows you to get straight to the

point which is important in a brief intervention.

CLIENT: "The place in Alaska when I was by myself."

STUDENT COACH: "Can you describe it in detail for me?"

CLIENT: "Well, I'm by a river with my dog. It was the first time I ever skied across the river. I felt anxiety, fear, doubt, excitement because I wasn't sure how frozen it was and if the ice would hold me."

STUDENT COACH: "Alright, so looking at the river, ask the river what's your purpose?"

INSTRUCTOR: I prefer to be more invitational. For example, "If you are comfortable doing this…." Or, "I invite you to ask the river."

CLIENT: "Following the change. It is solid, and it's changing. Trusting I'll make the right decision, trusting it'll hold."

STUDENT COACH: "Ask the river if it can show you a tangible way that you can trust it?"

INSTRUCTOR: Again, this feels too directive.

CLIENT: "The river is just solid, and I crossed it! Now I'm in the woods on the other side of the river, and I can cross it anytime I want to."

STUDENT COACH: "Now that you're in the forest what does it feel and look like here?"

CLIENT: "This is my comfort zone. This is recognizable like all the places I've been. It's not moving… it's still… it's winter… it's peaceful."

INSTRUCTOR: Time permitting, you could let the client savor the peace— there's no need to rush into words.

STUDENT COACH: "What do you see when you look around?"

CLIENT: "I see a trail. It's winter; it's muted. There are trees and there's a path."

STUDENT COACH: "What happens when you focus on the path?"

CLIENT: "I want to see where it goes. It feels easier. I do have these thoughts that maybe I should turn around, but this feels so peaceful, so recognizable."

STUDENT COACH: "Do you have any other thoughts or images as you stand here?"

CLIENT: "It's just myself and my dog. I'm just responsible for myself."

STUDENT COACH: "Take in a couple of deep breaths and breathe out, allowing yourself to stay in this moment of just being responsible for yourself. Be in this time of winter, of turning inward, of reflection.

As the time for our session comes to a close, I'd like you to gently come back into this present moment and come back to this intention: what's the best path for all of us? Remembering that we started in the winter and Alaska when it was a time before you had kids and you were skiing by yourself, and you had to cross a river that was still flowing underneath, but you didn't know if it was solid. And you made it across into this comfort zone and beautiful stillness, this recognizable place where "I'm just responsible for myself" and the relief that you felt as you spoke about it. What are your insights from this image?"

CLIENT: "I think you hit the nail on the head. I think before I can make any decisions I need to be responsible for myself and maybe start looking inward and taking a little bit of time for myself. How do I do that?"

STUDENT COACH: "So here are some coaching activities that we can work on …."

INSTRUCTOR: Here, I would first ask the client what she thinks would be helpful; after exploring her ideas, you might then offer suggestions of your own, but don't cut short the client's process of discovery. It is important that you co-create next steps and the time-frame in which they should be accomplished.

CLIENT: "Thank you so much for your time; thank you so much for these insights; I look forward to talking more about this."

STUDENT COACH: "Thank you for sharing."

BRIEF SUMMARY REGARDING THE EFFECTIVENESS OF THE SESSION. STRENGTHS? WHAT WOULD YOU DO DIFFERENTLY? CLIENT FEEDBACK, IF ANY?

STUDENT COACH: I think it went well, given the time constraint. I try keeping a good boundary on time if I see something is going to take a certain amount of time. At the end of the session, we looked at some activities and ways to turn inward that the client could do in her busy, practical life. The client found this helpful.

I don't tend to feel very smooth with the first interaction with the image in any of my practice sessions. Is there a standard question we could ask the image to get the interaction started and provide a solid starting point?

INSTRUCTOR: I think you did fine. Remember that in a coaching context you wouldn't start out with imagery but with the client's agenda. Then, if Image Guidance seems appropriate, you could briefly explain the process and ask the client if he or she would be open to this. The more you practice the process, the easier it will be to frame questions and to use the client's own imagery to provide guidance.

***

Each of the sample student transcripts represents a coach's first efforts at incorporating **Image Guidance** into a life coaching session; as assignments, it is to be expected that the transcripts will reflect some awkwardness at first. In some cases, the coaches are too directive; in others, there is an absence of descriptive detail and the sessions seem rushed. All in all, however, these were great efforts, and, with practice, all the coaches involved have the potential to acquire fluency with this tool.

APPENDIX ONE:
COACHING CLIENT'S INTAKE FORM

Since **Image Guidance** is a powerful way of accessing the unconscious and since material from all of one's life can surface unexpectedly during the process, it is important that your coach should be familiar with your medical history. Please be honest in your responses so that s/he can determine whether brief, non-therapeutic imagery interventions might occasionally be an appropriate part of your coaching experience:

NAME:

ADDRESS:

CELL PHONE:

EMAIL ADDRESS:

OCCUPATION:

EMPLOYER:

BIRTH DATE:

REFERRAL SOURCE:

EMERGENCY CONTACT:

CELL PHONE:

EMAIL ADDRESS

HEALTHCARE PROVIDERS:

Name: Phone:

Role:

Name: Phone:

Role:

In the event of an emergency, do I have your permission to contact your healthcare providers?　Yes_____　No_____

Medications you are currently taking:

Health problems, if any:

_____

1. What makes you willing to try brief experiences of **Image Guidance** during life coaching?

2. What are your expectations of the process?

3. Have you ever worked with imagery before? If so, with what results?

4. Have you discussed **Image Guidance** with your Healthcare Providers? If so, do they approve?

5. Are you presently in therapy? If so, have you discussed **Image Guidance** with your therapist? Does s/he approve of this process?

6. Do you have a history of depression? If so, have you ever been hospitalized for depression or been on medication for depression? Please provide details.

7. Did you experience any childhood traumas which still cause you pain or unhappiness?

8. Have you experienced any traumas in adult life which still evoke pain and unhappiness?

9. Is there any other information which will help your coach decide whether **Image Guidance** would be a safe and effective tool in your work together?

10. What aspects of your life are presently working well?

11. What aspects of your life could be improved?

12. Why are you seeking life coaching at this time?

I, _____, understand that **Image Guidance** is a tool for accessing the unconscious and for unlocking one's own inner wisdom. Though in life coaching the purpose of **Image Guidance** is non-therapeutic, painful material may sometimes surface unexpectedly.

I also understand that neither life coaching nor **Image Guidance** replaces conventional medical interventions, but, instead, complements them. It has been made very clear to me that neither life coaching nor **Image Guidance** is a form of therapy nor a substitute for medical examination and diagnosis. I also understand that I should not discontinue any form of physical or psychological treatment without first consulting my healthcare providers.

I understand that life-changing decisions may result from life coaching and **Image Guidance** and therefore take full responsibility for any decisions I make as a result of this process.

With this in mind, I hold my life coach harmless regarding any problems or difficulties that may surface as a result of our work together.

SIGNATURE_____ DATE_____

PRINTED NAME_____

APPENDIX TWO:
COACHING ASSESSMENT FORM

As you begin using **Image Guidance** with your clients, you may find it helpful to spend some time reflecting on each session. As you become more familiar with the process, it will feel more "natural" and such reflection will be unnecessary. Here are some guiding questions to get you started:

NAME OF CLIENT: DATE:

1. What imagery manifested during the coaching session?

2. How did the imagery reflect the client's coaching agenda?

3. What made you decide to focus on imagery during the coaching session?

4. What did you hope to accomplish by focusing on the client's use of imagery?

5. Did you ask the client for permission to work with imagery during the session?

6. Was the client open to the use of imagery?

7. Did you explain the process to the client or was there no need to do so?

8. Did you prepare the client for imagery work through breathing exercises or was this unnecessary?

9. What specific imagery did you focus on and why?

10. Was the client able to describe his or her primary image in depth?

11. How did your client respond to your use of **Image Guidance**?

12. Did the client have a conversation with his or her primary image? If so, what was the outcome?

13. Were there any physical or emotional shifts in your client following the use of imagery?

14. Did you experience any physical or emotional shifts while working with this client?

15. Did your client find insight, comfort, motivation, support or other benefits following the use of imagery?

16. Did your use of **Image Guidance** advance the client's agenda and, if so, how?

17. How did you bring the imagery experience to closure?

18. What "worked" regarding your use of **Image Guidance?**

19. What could you have done differently?

20. How would you evaluate the experience?

21. How did the client respond to **Image Guidance?**

22. What was the client's "take away"?

23. Will you use **Image Guidance** with this client again?

24. What have you learned in terms of **Image Guidance** techniques that you will be able to use next time you work with a client?

WORKS CITED

Achterberg, Jean. *Imagery in Healing: Shamanism and Modern Medicine.* Boston, MA: New Science Library, 1985.

Barrett, Richard. *A New Psychology of Human Well-Being: An Exploration of the Influence of Ego-Soul Dynamics on Mental and Physical Health.* London: 2016

Campbell, Joseph, ed. *The Portable Jung.* New York: Viking Penguin, Inc., 1971.

Cousins, Ewert. *Christ of the 21st Century.* Mass.: Element, Inc., 1992.

Goodell, Jeff. https://www.rollingstone.com/culture/news/bill-gates-the-rolling-stone-interview-20140313

Fowler, James W. *Stages of Faith.* New York: Harper Collins, 1995.

Hannah, Barbara. *Encounters with the Soul: Active Imagination as Developed by CG. Jung.* Boston, MA: Sigo Press, 1981.

Johnson, Robert A. *Inner Work: Using Dreams and Active Imagination for Personal Growth.* New York: Harper & Row, 1989.

Jung, C.G. *Man and His Symbols.* New York: Dell Publishers, 1964.

Greg J. Stephens, Lauren J. Silbert and Uri Hasson. *"Speaker–Listener Neural Coupling Underlies Successful Communication."* Proceedings of the National Academy of Sciences, Vol. 107 No. 29, July 27, 2010.

Stewart, Elizabeth-Anne. *Jesus the Holy Fool.* WI: Sheed & Ward, 1999.

Vanek (Stewart), Elizabeth-Anne. *Image Guidance and Healing.* New Jersey: Paulist Press, 1994.

Vanek (Stewart), Elizabeth-Anne. *Image Guidance: A Tool for Spiritual Direction.* New Jersey: Paulist Press, 1992.

Mind-Shifting Imagery

ABOUT
THE AUTHOR

Dr. Elizabeth-Anne Stewart

My Story in a Nutshell

Born in England and raised both in England and on the tiny Mediterranean island of Malta, I have always been a leader with multiple interests, inexhaustible energy and a delight in creativity. I love people and especially enjoy the roles of teacher and guide; nothing pleases me more than to be the midwife of an *"Ah Ha"* moment, a catalyst for meaningful change and for growth in awareness. Having transcended many personal challenges, assisted by amazing *Helpers Along the Way*, I am committed to sharing what I have learned through my writing and by offering coaching, retreats and seminars.

My Coaching Approach

As a faculty member for twenty-eight years at *DePaul University*, I was known as *"The Great Motivator,"* a quality that to this day remains the hallmark of my Life Coaching and other areas of professional life. I like to think of myself as constantly engaged in the Transformation of Consciousness— both my own and that of others. When we learn to see possibility instead of limitation, fullness instead of emptiness, abundance instead of lack, then we can tap into the inner well where all our wisdom resides. *We hold our own answers!*

Coaching Background

I have offered coaching/ spiritual direction since 1988-1989 when I trained as a spiritual director at the ***Claret Center***, Chicago; during that time, I developed a process of dialoguing with the unconscious that I named ***Image Guidance***, subsequently publishing two books on the topic with Paulist Press, NJ. As a University Minister at ***DePaul University***, I spent countless hours offering pastoral counseling, crisis intervention and facilitating groups around inner work topics. I also founded a training and formation program for spiritual directors serving the ***Archdiocese of Chicago, "Walking to Emmaus."***

Academic Background

The author of many books and articles, I am a member of *ICF* (The International Coach Federation) and *SDI* (Spiritual Directors International), I am on faculty at the *Institute for Life Coach Training* (ILCT) where I teach coaching courses with a spiritual focus; I also teach English at *St. Xavier University* and *Roosevelt University*. Trained as a Spiritual Director at the *Claret Center,* Chicago, I hold the BCC, a PhD in Theology (*University of Malta*), a Doctor of Ministry in Poetry (*Graduate Theological Foundation*), a B.A. in English (*University of Malta*), and an M.A. in English (*DePaul University*)

Professional Interests

Over the years, my range of professional ventures has included life coaching, spiritual direction, writing coaching, public speaking coaching, relationship coaching, healing with the imagination, photography, wedding officiating, motivational seminars and teaching Argentine Tango! Each of these seemingly unrelated activities demands full active listening, mindfulness, responsive presence, and positive regard for the client; the breadth and depth of these interests require flexibility, creativity and ongoing learning— all invaluable skills for any coach!

BOOKS

BY DR. ELIZABETH-ANNE STEWART

Preaching & Teaching Laudato Si'

Preaching and Teaching Laudato Si' is not a synopsis of Pope Francis' Encyclical on the Environment, but a simply written primer for those who wish to preach, teach or reflect on the spiritual implications of a green agenda; it is a resource for those of any faith who wish to respond to the Pope's plea for ecological conversion.

Available on Amazon in print and as a Kindle download.
ISBN-13: 978-1515378396
Print= $10:00; £6.43; €9.06
Kindle= $3.00

A Pocketful of Sundays

This book is a collection of scripturally-based reflections from my monthly e-letter, *Sunday BibleTalk.* It is a resource to be "dipped into" and read contemplatively, rather than read "cover to cover."

ISBN 5800030-792242
Print= $16.00. Please contact the author.

The Day the Fireworks Died

It is the *festa* of San Gorg, but dark clouds hang over the village of Ta' Qalbi and none of the fireworks will ignite. Gorg, a village outcast known to his schoolmates as "Hushu Bushu," learns from San Gorg that the saint is displeased with the people of Ta'Qalbi who, though church-going, are heartless and corrupt. With the help of Id Dragun, the dragon, Gorg confronts the people of his village and there is a change of heart all around -- as well as fireworks, processions and marching bands..... A parable for children 10-14 and adults.

Malta, PEG Publications, 2005
ISBN 99909-0-379-4
Print= $10.00. Please contact the author.

The Maltese Translation/Adaptation, ID-DRAGUN TAD-DRAGONARA, released in 2017, is available from Preca Publications, Malta: https://issuu.com/preca

Dragut's Galley

Two young American teenagers visit their grandparents in Malta, a Mediterranean island with a history of repeated invasions by Turkish corsairs. Excited by the legends of this historic past, they set out to discover their roots and discover a deeper truth than they ever imagined... Set in contemporary Malta, the author's homeland and sacred landscape, *Dragut's Galley*, is an adventure story intended for readers 9-14 years of age, as well as for adults who are children at heart; it delivers a positive message much needed in a world divided by religious differences and intolerance.

Malta, PEG Publications, 2004
ISBN 99909-0-379-4
Print= $10.00. Please contact the author.

Jesus the Holy Fool

My best-known book is *Jesus the Holy Fool* (Wisconsin: Sheed & Ward, 1999). This is a reverent study of the Gospel Jesus which draws connections between holiness and folly as they occur in the bible, presenting Holy Foolishness as a paradigm for the Christian journey and as a new model for what it means to be church. In 1999, this book caused controversy in South Africa where politicians who misunderstood the meaning of "Holy Fool" wanted to ban the 1999 *Parliament of the World's Religions* because of my presentation on this topic. Ela Gandhi, granddaughter of Mahatma Gandhi, and Gordon Oliver, former mayor of Cape Town, came to my defense. The African National Democratic Party later apologized in the South African Parliament; protests, however, continued throughout the *Parliament of the World's Religions*.

"Brings to light ancient wisdom about the mystery of Christ. Reverent and challenging."
Donald Senior, C.P., **Catholic Theological Union**

"Combines sound theology with creative imagination. Enlightens and delights."
Marie-Henry Keane, O.P., **Blackfriars Hall, Oxford University**

"A wise, rich, and theologically informed book; a moving invitation to consider an important new dimension of Christology."
Wayne G. Rollins, **Hartford Seminary**

Wisconsin: Sheed & Ward, 1999
ISBN: 1-58051-061-2
Order from https://rowman.com/ or try Amazon.com

From Center to Circumference:
God's Place in the Circle of Self

This book offers a series of brief reflections on the inner life, drawing on my own experiences as a means of illustration. Not meant as mere autobiography, these reflections point beyond personal narrative to universal wisdom. The book can serve as a journaling tool or as a "manual for spiritual direction."

"Those who read this book will be provoked to gather, reverence and share their own stories of grace."
Louis J. Cameli, **University of St. Mary of the Lake**

"Her wisdom, enhanced by many years as a spiritual director, shines through. The reader will feel the sure and gentle touch of her guiding hand."
Ewert Cousins, **Fordham University**

New Jersey: Paulist Press, 1996
ISBN 0-8091-3623-6
Presently out of print.

Image Guidance and Healing

Stressing the inter-connectedness of body-mind-spirit, the book provides a variety of case studies which illustrate the use of **Image Guidance** in post-accident rehabilitation, in stress-related illnesses, in serious conditions such as diabetes and cancer, in addictions and in minor ailments with a psycho-spiritual basis.

"Vanek's case material provides an excellent embodiment of the image guidance process and helps the reader to appreciate the very real gift she brings to this endeavor."
Joan E. Bowers, ***Department of Nursing, DePaul University***

"Elizabeth-Anne Vanek is an intuitive healer with an uncanny ability to help her clients express and transform their physical problems through imagery. Extending Jung's technique of active imagination, a type of inner dialogue with spontaneous images, she illustrates how to evoke this healing fantasy in individuals with physiological conditions."
August J. Cwik, ***Jung Institute, Evanston***

New Jersey: Paulist Press, 1994
ISBN 0-8091-3508-6
Presently out of print.

Image Guidance: A Tool for Spiritual Direction

Through a series of case studies, I demonstrate how to dialogue with the active imagination so as to use imagery as an intuitive map that will help guide our lives. The book provides a step by step account of how to work with the spontaneous image, how to extract wisdom from our dreams and how to recognize the symbolic significance of mythical themes.

"For those who are attracted by their imaginations to the way of symbols, Elizabeth-Anne Vanek's book offers a privileged access to those symbols that emerge from the depths of the psyche and with grace and guidance can lead the spiritual pilgrim toward the goal of the journey."
Ewert Cousins, ***Fordham University***

New Jersey: Paulist Press, 1992
ISBN:0-8091-3321-0
Print= $16.00. Please contact the author.

Pilgrims at Heart

This pocket book offers some of my best scripture reflections from *Living Faith*, a quarterly publication which provides brief meditations on the day's readings. From 1985-2005, I wrote the Sunday reflections for *Living Faith*, offering insights that came from lived experience rather than from mere book learning.

"As a person convinced of the truth of faith, Vanek writes with the urgency of one searching for a way to express that faith genuinely in her everyday life. Her insight into the spiritual journey can enrich all of us, no matter where we find ourselves on the pilgrimage to the heart of God."
The Editors, ***Living Faith Publications***

St. Louis: Creative Communications for the Parish, 1993
ISBN: 0-9629585-3-0;$7.50
To order: 1-800-325-9414

Woman Dreamer

This collection of poems is grounded in archetypal imagery. While some of the themes are distinctly Christian or are shaped by the Hebrew scriptures, still others draw on the world of myth, providing a new twist to stories of creation, fall and redemption. Many of the poems are mystical in orientation and focus on the relationship between Lover and Beloved, especially on the desire for union and the intense emotions that such yearning entails.

"The reader who follows Vanek's guidance through scenes of everyday life, through the drama of Biblical narratives, and through the forest of primordial archetypal symbols, will be delighted aesthetically and enriched spiritually."
Ewert Cousins, *Fordham University*

Indiana: Wyndham Hall, 1989
ISBN-55605-126-3
Print= $8.00. Please contact the author.

Leaning Into Light

This collection of poetry brings together the best selections from *Frost and Fire* (Canton, Ohio: Life Enrichment Publishers, 1985) and *Extraordinary Time* (Life Enrichment Publishers, 1988). Both these books, which represent my earliest published work, are out of print; however, I do have multiple copies available of this volume. The poems trace much of my own spiritual journey.

"The most effective prophets are poets. They lead us to truth and goodness through the beautiful. Elizabeth-Anne Vanek is such a prophet. Her poetry helps us to hear the biblical stories anew, to see their settings and to enter into the very flesh and spirit of those who move about seeking God. She helps us to pray biblical prayers, to hear biblical stories as our own stories, and to delight in biblical wisdom as though it were all our own discovery."
Eugene LaVerdiere, SSS

"I am again impressed with the delicate touch of beauty and the intense movement of contemplation in your work. I thank you for sharing this gift with us."
Carroll Stuhlmueller, C.P.

"These poems are like favorite melodies transposed into a minor key, haunting the reader with the intimate revelations of the actors, their sudden recognition of the overwhelming presence of God; This book is a very powerful acclamation that sign-seeking is universal, and that waiting for what is possible, sometimes in frustration, is worthwhile."
Linda McCallum Krause, Reviewer, *Currents in Theology and Mission*

Print= $5.00. Please contact the author.

Made in the
USA
Columbia, SC